What peo

Being a Supervisor 1.0

Being a Supervisor 1.0 is a must read for everyone involved in staff training and organizational development. Whether you are a newly promoted supervisor, manager or an experienced human resource trainer, you will greatly benefit from this book. Joe Duffy has provided a comprehensive review of all aspects of the important role that supervisors play in our work settings. I highly recommend reading this book to everyone involved in leadership and supervision.

Dennis C. Miller, Executive Search, Author, Speaker, Leadership Coach

Being a Supervisor 1.0 is not only an invaluable primer for any employee or first-time supervisor aspiring to be an outstanding manager of people, but it is an excellent reference for seasoned and experienced supervisors and managers as a refresher course as well. It is a compact, comprehensive, grassroots manual on the correct way to manage people, projects, and progress, and I highly recommend it to all in pursuit of supervisory excellence.

Bettina A. Deynes, MBA, MIM, SHRM-SCP, IPMA-CP; VP of Human Resources and Diversity; Society for Human Resource Management (SHRM); co-author of *Alejandra's Quest*; international presenter and published author on leadership, management and HR topics

Supervision is both an art and a science. It can be learned but must be practiced to be fully mastered. Good supervision skills are especially important for the civil society/nonprofit sector which relies greatly on influence and collaboration. They are essential too for the government and business sectors. In *Being a Supervisor 1.0* Joe Duffy sets out easy to understand foundational

management knowledge that every supervisor needs. These practical lessons, learned from a long career and leadership, are timely for the 21st century manager in any and all sectors.
M.D. Kinoti, PhD, Associate Professor of Nonprofit Management, Regis University, Colorado, International NGO Consultant

Strong organizations all have one thing in common: skilled, effective supervisors, passionate about mission. Joe Duffy has delivered a terrific toolbox for new or aspiring supervisors, as well as more seasoned leaders keen to learn from another's experience. Joe's half a century of education and experience percolate throughout this excellent and informative handbook.
Kevin Ryan, President of Covenant House and former Commissioner, New jersey department of Children and Families

Being a Supervisor 1.0 is an excellent must-read resource for considering foundational management issues. Utilizing a quick-read format, Joe Duffy shares his lessons learned over a 45 year career, providing not only practical advice, but also many "tools" for managing. But, perhaps of most value, are the numerous questions that the reader is presented with, as these should help the reader to translate Mr. Duffy's experiences and suggestions into the reader's own supervisory approach.
Terrence Cahill, EdD, FACHE, Department Chair and Associate Professor Department of Interprofessional Health Sciences and Health Administration Seton Hall University, Consultant, Leadership Coach

Joe Duffy's *Being a Supervisor* 1.0 is an essential handbook for supervisors of the future who will need this wisdom, to be effective supervisors today and tomorrow.
Frances Hesselbein, President & CEO, The Frances Hesselbein Leadership Institute

Joe Duffy draws on a long, varied executive career to provide an intelligent, interesting road map for new and experienced supervisors. The writing is vivid, direct and practical; the wisdom of his advice pervades this useful contribution from a successful, seasoned leader.

J. Bryan Hehir, Secretary for Social Service, Archdiocese of Boston; Past President CCUSA

Being a Supervisor 1.0 is a very practical reference guide for both seasoned managers and new supervisors, or for anyone with leadership responsibilities. The book contains excellent suggestions on ways leaders can embrace change. Joe Duffy provides first-rate recommendations that enable managers to work within different personalities and management styles. This book is a must read for anyone interested in management training.

Kevin Lynch, Senior Consultant, IC Consulting

Being a Supervisor 1.0 is a must read for the first time or aspiring supervisor and as a useful tool for the experienced supervisor. Author Joe Duffy has compiled lessons learned from a 45 year career in management into one easy to read handbook. It will be your "go to" resource for help in dealing with the daily demands of being a supervisor.

Thomas J. Healey, Partner Healey Development, Board Member Leadership Roundtable, Senior Fellow Harvard University JFK School of Government, Former Assistant Secretary of the US Treasury for Domestic Finance

The rate of change in leadership at not-for-profit agencies is occurring at a pace never before seen. Joe Duffy has presented a highly readable and personable road-map for new CEOs to front line supervisors as they seek to avoid running around on the organizational shoals.

Richahrd Klarberg, JD, President & CEO, Council on Accreditation

I highly recommend reading *Being a Supervisor 1.0*! The book has structure, purpose and practical concepts for leaders and managers. New and seasoned supervisors will benefit from it. Get your copy.

James D Raphael, LNHA,CALA,MBA; President and CEO, James Raphael Enterprises

Well articulated and very informative book *Becoming a Supervisor 1.0* written by Joe Duffy provides the essential tools for a new supervisor as well as a handbook for the seasoned supervisor.

Mukunda Panuganti, MS, PHR, SHRM-CP; Human Resources Director

Being a
Supervisor 1.0

Being a Supervisor 1.0

Joseph F. Duffy

**BUSINESS
BOOKS**

Winchester, UK
Washington, USA

First published by Business Books, 2018
Business Books is an imprint of John Hunt Publishing Ltd., No. 3 East St., Alresford,
Hampshire SO24 9EE, UK
office1@jhpbooks.net
www.johnhuntpublishing.com

For distributor details and how to order please visit the 'Ordering' section on our website.

ISBN: 978 1 78535 792 3
978 1 78535 793-0 (ebook)
Library of Congress Control Number: 2017947284

A CIP catalogue record for this book is available from the British Library.

Design: Cecilia Perriard

Printed and bound by CPI Group (UK) Ltd, Croydon, CR0 4YY, UK

We operate a distinctive and ethical publishing philosophy in
all areas of our business, from our global network of authors to
production and worldwide distribution.

Contents

Acknowledgements

I want to acknowledge and thank my wife Carolyn and our children, Kevin, Megan and Ryan for not only tolerating my workaholic personality, but for supporting me and those traits throughout my career, even now, in some of the volunteer work I am doing in retirement. The experience and knowledge learned at work, in school, and serving on non-profit, government and for-profit boards was source material for most of this manuscript.

I am grateful for my colleagues (in alpha order) Robert Bozzomo, Scott Milliken, Anita Morawski, Dharmesh Parikh, Philomena Pereira, James Raphael, and Reina Rivas. They helped create the positive work environment I espouse in this book. They helped me grow as a leader. And very importantly, each of them reviewed at least one of the chapters of my manuscript. I offer special thanks to my colleague and friend, Anita Morawski, who reviewed almost this entire work. She questioned some of it; corrected grammar, punctuation, and spelling; and offered stylistic suggestions. The final product was much improved because of her help.

At my retirement dinner, my long time executive assistant, Cathy Spina, also retired, told me to call her anytime. I called. Thanks Cathy for creating some of the forms I used in this book.

The decision-making drawings in Chapter 7 are the creation of my nephew, Josh Burke. I can't even draw stick figures, Thanks much Josh. Thanks too, to Josh, and his dad, John, for their advice on using social media as a tool for marketing this book.

I thank Richard G. Lazar, PhD., Chairman Emeritus of the Lazar Group who first introduced me to the win-win approach to conflict resolution when he provided management consultation services at St. Joseph's Hospital in Paterson in the late 1970s. The win-win approach remains my preferred approach to conflict management today. Dr. Lazar was so kind as to review the outline for this book and offer suggestions and resources.

Thank you to the endorsers who despite their own demanding schedules took the time to read this manuscript and commend it to you.

And last, but certainly not least, I thank John Hunt Publishing for taking a chance on this first time author and your editing, publishing, graphic design and marketing staff for their expertise and support.

Introduction

Throughout my 45 year career in management, I have consistently described myself as a professional student. That includes not just the learning I've done in traditional educational settings, but the learning that happens on the job, as well as the active practice of continuous reading of books and journals. Much of that reading has been, and still is, on the subject of leadership and supervision. I've often recommended these works to my direct reports, but in all my searching for pertinent material, never have I come across a single book that covers all the topics a supervisor needs to know to be successful in his/her role. Given the management skills that I have developed over the years, it has occurred to me that perhaps I should write that missing book, a handbook that encompasses the breadth and depth of what it takes to be an effective supervisor. I am retired now, though I continue to do some consulting and training in the field. I'm also still that professional student, exploring all the resources available. Finally, I decided that maybe it's time to contribute to that collection of resources, and write my own book.

This book is written for two audiences. The primary audience is the first-time (and aspiring) supervisor. Most first time supervisors are line staff, promoted because of good performance. The assumption is that a good employee will make a good supervisor. But that is not necessarily the case. The two roles carry vastly different responsibilities, and without proper preparation, a stellar employee can fail miserably as a supervisor. It takes some combination of classes, reading, workshops, on-the-job training, and ongoing supervision, to successfully transition from staff to supervisor. This book is my effort to take my years of experience and education and codify it into a single source document that can assist the new supervisor in making that transition, and developing his or her supervisory skills.

The second audience is for experienced supervisors. Learning is a lifelong process. Even seasoned supervisors can benefit, learn and grow in their position. In my years of overseeing multi-million dollar agencies, I haven't known one supervisor who didn't at times face complicated situations and need extra guidance in managing them. It was often the most "veteran" supervisors, those who had become rigid in their habits, who could have most benefited from new and different ideas in dealing with their complex operations. This book will offer them the opportunity to consider methods that, in my experience, are indispensable for dealing with the most mundane to the most obscure.

I recommend, especially for the first-time supervisor, that you read the book once, cover to cover. Then go back and read those chapters that deal with a topic of particular interest to you. Keep the book handy and re-read chapters from time to time as that subject matter becomes an area of need or concern, or just as a refresher.

Have you ever heard the three envelopes joke? I was unable to identify the joke's creator but found the joke reprinted in *The Huffington Post* June 29, 2012. On his way out, the outgoing manager hands the new manager three envelopes and remarks, "When things get tough, open these one at a time."

About three months go by and things start to get rough. the manager opens his drawer where he keeps the three envelopes and opens #1. It reads: "Blame your predecessor." So he does and it works like a charm.

Another three months pass and things are growing difficult again so the manager figures to try #2. It reads, "Reorganize." Again, his predecessor's advice works like magic.

Finally, about nine months into the new job, things are getting really sticky. The manager figures it worked before, why not try again. So he opens the envelope drawer one last time and opens #3. It reads…"Prepare three envelopes."

It is a joke, but sadly, it is all too often reality for new supervisors, unprepared for the job. Be prepared. Read this handbook and keep it handy, at least until a better one comes out.

Chapter 1

Vetting the Organization

Be Prepared

Were you ever a Boy or Girl Scout? Scouts are guided by The Scout Motto, Scout Slogan, Scout Oath, and Scout Law. I learned them over 50 years ago and can still recite them word for word. I am proud to say I am guided by them even today. For those who are unfamiliar, and for others who are familiar but can't quite recall, The Scout Motto is "Be Prepared." That is sound advice in all aspects of life and certainly for any supervisor.

A corollary phrase to the Scout Motto is the proverb *"Forewarned is forearmed."* One of the earliest documented references to it, is in a letter dated 1685 from Captain Francis Hooke, advising of the dangers of frontier life in the Americas. This letter appeared in John Farmer's *The History of New Hampshire in 1831.* The proverb was prefaced with the phrase "A word to the wise is enough; the old proverb is forewarned, forearmed."

For emphasis, I would combine the motto and the proverb as follows: *Be prepared; forewarned is forearmed.* If you seek or welcome being forewarned, you can be forearmed, and so, be prepared. While this advice is important for preparation before your first day of work it is also equally useful every day at work. So how can you "Be Prepared" before the first reporting day?

Go Surfing

Before starting a job, you want to be sure there is congruence and compatibility, between your own personal and professional goals and values and the Mission, Vision and Values of the Organization, and that you are comfortable in embracing them and working in a manner consistent with them. If there is not such congruence your work with the organization will likely be unhappy, unproductive, and short-lived, and could even create a toxic work environment. Visit the organization's website (presuming there is one). It is common for most organizations, public, private, government, for-profit and non-profit, to have one. If you are unable to find one, that might be an indication of an organization that does not keep up with the times, slow to change. Certainly inquire if there is one during the interview process if you have not already found one. Surf the website to learn as much as you can about the organization, its history, current operations, program summaries, brochures, future plans, leadership, annual report, and financial condition.

Ask Human Resources (HR)

If there is no web site, you can certainly ask the contact person at the organization or the HR director there for such items and ask questions you might have after reading them. Don't take it for granted that you will be presented with a job description during the interview process. If you are not, be sure to ask for one. I cannot tell you how often I have been told by an employee, including a supervisory level employee, that he or she did not know all his/ her duties prior to starting work, and were shocked when they learned all they were expected to do after the starting day.

Read

Read the employee handbook, and if there is a separate personnel *policies and procedures* manual, read it sooner than later, hopefully before you start meeting employees. It will not necessarily make the book of the month club, but it will help you "Be Prepared" and may prevent you from having to back step later when answering employees' queries, only to learn that your answer is inconsistent with policy.

Read the Sacred Documents

I often refer to Mission, Vision, and Values Statements as "Sacred

Documents". I would include Strategic Plans too as Sacred Documents. My own 45 year career in management has been in faith-based organizations in the fields of Catholic Healthcare, Catholic Education, and Catholic Charities, and as such, referring to these and others documents as "Sacred Documents" seems understandable, but I do believe the term is equally appropriate for non-faith-based organizations. I don't remember when I started using this reference, whether I coined the use of those words or adopted them from another source. They make sense to me as a way of emphasizing their importance not only in faith-based organizations, but all categories of organizations, faith-based or not, for profit and non-profit, public and private. Webster's dictionary offers several definitions of "sacred". The one I particularly like to embrace in support of calling them Sacred Documents is "set apart for, and dedicated to some person, place, or sentiment... secured by a sense of justice against any defamation, violation, or intrusion; inviolate." These documents, if committed to, even reverenced, become the *"raison d'être"* for the organization, giving it meaning and direction, providing a lens through which to make management decisions, assuring steadfastness to Mission, remaining on track towards realizing Vision, utilizing organizational Values in working towards achieving that Vision, and remaining faithful to the Mission as guided by the Strategic Plan (if there is one). There are many definitions for these sacred documents. Let me define each in words that are meaningful to me as a leader.

Mission Statement
In as few words as possible, the Mission Statement explains why the organization exists, what its purpose is. I subscribe to Peter Drucker's admonition that a Mission Statement should fit on a tee shirt. His reasoning and mine is that the Mission Statement needs to be widely known. Ideally you and every employee, when asked what the Mission of the organization

is, should be able to answer that question. As such, shorter is better.

Vision Statement

A Vision Statement is a look into the future, perhaps five or ten years down the road. It answers the question "How would you want the organization described in that future time frame question mark?" It challenges the organization and its employees to action, to realize the Vision while remaining faithful to the Mission. When working with organizations in developing a Vision Statement, I suggest they think of it as if they were writing their obituary for five or ten years down the road. I tell them to consider what they want the readers to read about them and their accomplishments. And I conclude that exercise by telling them that very likely, there would be differences in their ten year hence obituary from what would be written about them in the present time. The differences between the present and that time in the future are what need to be addressed to realize the Vision.

Values Statement

A Values Statement is a statement of important principles, the beliefs that become the moral compass of the organization, steering decisions and actions, guiding the organization and its employees and board in service of the Mission, and in realizing its Vision. Oftentimes they become referred to as Core Values. The organization decides upon these values and what they mean to the organization. By way of example, some typical organizational values might include, honesty, excellence, transparency, service.

Strategic Plan

A Strategic Plan fits hand and glove with a Vision Statement. A Strategic Plan Document looks at that point in the future (the

Vision, three to five years down the road) and identifies goals and action steps needed to realize its Vision. The Strategic Plan becomes the organization's GPS system guiding it on the journey from the present situation to that future Vision.

Don't just read these sacred documents. Seek clarification of anything that seems unclear especially if it might be problematic for your own beliefs. These are documents which you as a supervisor will need to know, embrace, adopt as your own, educate others about, and champion.

Read Other Sacred Documents

Organizations have other documents which if you read, you will be better prepared. Some may have an organizational history. Some may have a business or operational plan. All should have founding documents like bylaws, certificates of incorporation or amended certificates of incorporation, charters. Depending on the level of the supervisory position you are interested in, you will want to review financial information such as current budget, audit, tax filings (990 for non-profits and 1065 or 1120 for for-profits). While 990s are public documents easily found on the Guidestar website, for-profit tax statements are not public documents. You could however visit the Dunn and Bradstreet (D&B) website and find a D&B report on both for-profit and non-profit organizations. Asking if such documents exist will evidence your interest in the organization, and, if you are provided them, will be useful in confirming your interest in the organization.

Ask the Boss

If possible, and it usually is possible, sit down with your boss before you start and ask what is the most pressing issue that he/she wants you to deal with; any deadlines looming, reports due, etc. If he/she is expecting you to do A, and not having been told, you decide to push B, or C, D or J, your working relationship with the boss could be off to a rocky start. So find out what the boss' needs are – Be Prepared. If the boss is open to talking, ask about your staff, their strengths and weaknesses, who are the go-to folks among them, who needs to be supervised more closely, longevity, open positions (and to his knowledge why they are open). And by the way, do not make the assumption that everything the boss tells you is 100% accurate. Be guided here by the words of Ronald Reagan, "Trust but verify". You should hope that what you are told and what you read is accurate; trust it is, but as much you can, verify. Again, forewarned is forearmed – Be Prepared!

Caveat Emptor!

Webster's dictionary defines caveat emptor thus: the principle that the buyer alone is responsible for checking the quality and suitability of goods before a purchase is made. Very likely you are looking to take on this job for the long term, intending to stay and grow. The Sacred Documents as well as all the other information you gather, will tell you a lot about the organization, its, purpose, priorities, values and culture. If you find them to be inconsistent with your own personal and professional goals and values, think twice about taking the position. It is highly unlikely the organization will change its sacred documents to your liking.

Chapter 2

Look the Part

Dress for Success

Dress like a supervisor/manager. Look professional. Be a role model of dress code; neat, clean, well groomed.

The Duck Test

Have you heard of the Duck Test? "If it looks like a duck, quacks like a duck and walks like a duck, it's a duck." Take the lead from the first phrase of the test and look like a supervisor (DUCK). Dressing the part is not sufficient to be a supervisor (not a good one). But it is a necessary part. Appearances are not everything but they are important. If you don't look like a supervisor, you may be off to a shaky start with your direct reports, even with your boss. First impressions are important. Dressing like a supervisor will help you make a good first impression.

How to Pass the Duck Test

How does a supervisor dress? There is no one size fits all answer. Consider the organization's culture, and very likely, organizational policies concerning dress code and appearance. My eldest son was a senior development executive in a large NY non-profit. He would routinely wear slacks and a button down shirt to work and sneakers. I was surprised any organization would consider such as acceptable and questioned him. He assured me that the dress code was informal in his company for both staff and management. He also assured me when he was going out to a meeting or hosting a meeting for outsiders, the shirt, tie, jacket, and shoes came out. If you have been promoted from within, you will likely already have your answer, but even so, confirm. If you are new to the organization, you need to find out. It could be as simple as asking your supervisor what is the expected dress code, or ask the HR director/interviewer. If you are reluctant to ask point blank you can ask for a copy of the employee handbook, and or, a copy of the organization's employee policies and procedures to review and become acquainted with prior to the first day of work. Some employers will actually require you to read these documents prior to starting work and ask you to sign off acknowledging that you read them. In asking for such documents you can show your desire to fit in and be a team player by saying you want to be sure you are aware of key policies like dress code, work reporting requirements, for your own edification, and so you can assist your direct reports in meeting same. Asking such a question may even impress your boss and help get you off to a better start.

Trust and Verify

Reading the handbook or policies and procedures may not be sufficient. The information might be vague and open to interpretation. Some policies may be as a short as "dress professionally" or "business casual" and as such be wide open to interpretation (Google's policy is "you must wear clothes"). If it is not clear, ask for clarity, and ask of someone in authority to be sure you get the answer from those that will hold you accountable. Early on, confirm if the practice is consistent with what you read, and or, were told. In many organizations, acceptable dress has become more informal. It is not unusual that policies have remained unchanged, even though the practice has. You may make a judgment call and dress like the other management staff when you observe a difference between policy and practice, or you might again check in with your supervisor, point out your observation, and ask for clarification.

Looking Good

What you wear is important. So too is how you wear it and how you appear. Always remember, you are a role model. You will be expected to hold your direct reports accountable for compliance with the organization's dress code. If you do not walk the talk on this matter, it is likely your employees will not either. They are more likely to do what you do rather than what you say when you do not walk this talk.

Be sure your clothes are clean, pressed (or at least wrinkle free), and fit. Footwear too should be clean and polished. Hair should comply with the organization's policy, and it too should be clean and well kept. Maintain a high standard of personal hygiene and grooming too. Body art may need to be camouflaged and jewelry, practical. Cologne and perfume too needs to be considered. Even if policy does not address it, be aware that co-workers may be sensitive to odors, even allergic, and many work environments may be so environmentally controlled that even a modest amount of such may easily circulate through the HVAC system to the irritation of many. Clothes and how you wear them help to make the supervisor. Make that good first impression.

Have You Heard This One?

Changed HR Policies

Week 14 - Memo No. 6

The Casual Day Task Force has now completed a 30-page manual entitled "Relaxing Dress Without Relaxing Company Standards." A copy has been distributed to every employee. Please review the chapter "You Are What You Wear" and consult the "home casual" versus "business casual" checklist before leaving for work each Friday. If you have doubts about the appropriateness of an item of clothing, contact your CDTF representative before 7 a.m. on Friday.

Source: Aha! Jokes, http://www.AhaJokes.com/

Chapter 3

Meet and Greet and Get to Know

Essential to building a good working relationship with your staff is getting to know them and have them get to know you. There is no one right way to do this. Deciding how to do this must be determined by your own personal preference, the organization's policy or preferences, and logistics like time and space. It is a continuous process that should begin no later than the first day of work (sooner if you have the time and the organization has the time and interest).

Introduction

I want to share my approach to this topic as I assumed my last CEO position. With the permission and support of my predecessor a meet and greet meeting of all the supervisory staff was called. I introduced myself, shared my educational and work experience. I told them what I knew about their Mission, Vision and Values (had copies of same for all in attendance). I assured them of my commitment to the organization and its sacred documents. I shared my hopes and expectations and described my management style. I then went around the room asking them to tell me about themselves, their name, title, how long with the agency and any pressing need (realizing that in a first meeting some may be reluctant to fully share).

I recommend such a meet and greet, even if you are not new to the organization. Like it or not, things will change if you have been promoted from line to supervision. You are no longer one of the passengers in the car; you are the driver. You will need to behave differently. Some staff will already be wondering how you, their former peer, will be as their supervisor. So if you are not new to the organization, use this opportunity to introduce the new you.

Take Introduction on the Road

Following that initial meet and greet meeting, I took my act on the road for the remainder of that day and a few hours on two other days before I started on the job (but if this is not possible just do it at the earliest opportunity). I visited every program and site (across three counties). In some cases I was able to meet with entire departments as a group and went through the same meet and greet agenda as described above. In other cases I did it on my feet, meeting staff at work, and taking a few minutes for introductions, assuring them I would be back. Even with this effort I did not meet all the employees on these three days. Some employees were off when I visited. Some programs covered two shifts and some covered three shifts. I did visit all programs on all shifts at least once in my first 30 days on the job (and I visited those shifts again and again during my three year tenure with the organization).

Invite Informal Reference Check on You

As part of this meet and greet process I invited staff to check me out. I worked only a short distance from this organization for the prior 37 years. I told them that very likely some staff knew people I worked with in my prior positions. I encouraged them to call and check me out and share what they found with their co-workers (I would caution you to think twice about doing this if you are uncertain of what folks might say).

Some type of meet and greet, perhaps as described above, or some adaptation or combination of what was just described is a good start in "getting to know you". But it is just that, a start. It's actually a never ending process as people in the jobs change, new people come into the job place, and the work environment is always changing.

One-on-One or Small Group Follow-Up

The above meetings and contacts are the first step to meet and greet. What might be the second? Again, there is no one right answer but I will offer my usual approach. My preferred step two is to sit down one on one with my direct reports. I met with each of them in their office if they have one or privately in their workplace if they did not have an office. Meeting in my office would, I believe reinforce the power of the office. While it is understood they all work for me, my own style is that we work together and so I look for that first meeting in a setting that might be more comfortable for them. These are occasions for a rehash of the initial meet and greet but with more opportunity to get to know them better, find out what their needs are, and how I can assist them in support of our Mission and in support of their professional growth. This becomes the first of our regularly scheduled meetings. I prefer to meet with direct reports once a month on a scheduled basis individually and as a group. I'm not one to meet just for the sake of meeting but want to be certain we communicate regularly (so sometimes these meetings are very short). In addition to these scheduled meetings, I let staff know I am always available as needed (open-door policy).

Conduct Your Own Reference Checks

Prior to a first individual meeting with your direct reports you may want to review each person's personnel file. Some choose not to do so reasoning they might be biased by what they read, preferring instead to meet them uninformed by such content. For those who choose to go into that meeting cold, I recommend reading the file after the fact. If it confirms your first impression, then, all the better. If it doesn't confirm your first impression it becomes food for thought for ongoing supervision. If you read the file first and see a different version of the person in your first interview, that too is food for thought in ongoing supervision. In fact, if there are inconsistencies between your first meeting impressions and first file review impressions, you might want to discuss same with your boss. Guided by the Scout Motto and

Forewarned – Forearmed proverb, I prefer the read the file first approach.

Whether you review your direct reports personnel files before or after your first individual meeting, if you follow my advice in the Scout Motto chapter you would already have some background on them from having asked your boss about the strengths and weaknesses of your staff. Let me give you a tip right now, that I will say more about in a later chapter. Pay particular attention to employee performance reviews. In the chapter on supervision I will talk about them from the perspective of are they fact or fiction, or some combination.

MBWA

I have, for as long as I can remember, managed by the MBWA (management by walking/wandering around) method. I spend a portion of each day walking the place, being visible to staff and clients. After two months in my last position, one staff member complimented me saying she saw more of me in the last eight weeks than she had my predecessor in the last eight years. In my first year at Catholic Charities in 1997 I put 27,000 miles on my car driving among the 60 sites Catholic Charities operated in three contiguous counties. I introduce MBWA here as a means to get to know the organization and its staff. In addition though, MBWA is a useful tool for ongoing management.

I adapted the MBWA method slightly, adding to it "walk in my shoes". I really do want to know my team. Over the years in different positions, I have worked alongside maintenance and housekeeping staff painting rooms, shoveling snow, and cleaning bathrooms. I greeted and registered patients alongside registration staff in our clinics and doctors' offices; processed discharge paper in the E.R. with clerks there, shaved, fed and bathed residents of our nursing home alongside the nursing assistants and acted as an agency driver transporting clients. MBWA in general and through the special tasks just described served several purposes. It gave me a better idea of what the organization was about, its strengths and weaknesses. It helped me remain keenly aware of the work environment, its appearance, and repair, and morale. It helped me to get to know staff and build a relationship with them. It helped me to get and keep my finger on the pulse of the organization.

Some people think they know their organization. I believe a robust use of MBWA as described above will assure that you really do know the organization. Let me offer this story as proof. When I worked at St. Joseph's Regional Medical Center I served for a period of five years as the administrator of their nursing home. One day one of the nursing assistants came to see me (open-door policy). She wanted to share the news that a union was asking her co-workers to sign a petition to organize and that she was unhappy about that. I told her that employees had the legal and moral right to organize and that I would not impede any effort, stating too that I thought employees trusted my leadership and were comfortable sharing any concerns directly with me rather than through a third party. When I reported the matter to the Hospital CEO, she brought in a labor attorney to help prepare and to educate me and management staff on how to conduct ourselves and avoid any unfair labor practices. Part of his consultation was a recommendation to stall any election date. I was concerned about the stress in the work environment that might accompany any delay in the election and I was confident I knew staff. I was certain that there was little interest in unionizing. I told the attorney I would welcome an early election date, confident of the outcome. He was cautious though and recommended we wait and see if the union produced sufficient signatures to schedule an election. Within a matter of weeks the union went away, apparently unable to secure even close to enough signatures to force an election. MBWA helped me call this right. (Please do not construe this example as offering my opinion pro or con union. I believe employees have the right to organize. I also believe that management has the obligation to treat employees fairly and when they do, employees will feel comfortable with and prefer to deal directly with management rather than through an outside intermediary).

MBWA Case Example

As the Administrative Director for Ambulatory Care at St. Joseph's Regional Medical Center I was responsible for administrative support of the Emergency Room. I practiced the MBWA method regularly. One day the Vice President for nursing called and asked if I could stop by her office to discuss something. When I arrived she told me that her ER head nurse called and said "He was here again, the third time this week." I learned from that experience that my presence which was intended to show support for the staff was actually making them nervous, wondering what I was looking for, or who I was trying to catch doing something wrong. As a result I met one-on-one with the head nurse and then with her nursing staff as a group to better get to know them, explain my management philosophy (especially MBWA). Things were much better after that, and soon after, nursing staff felt comfortable calling me to come down to see something or to help with a problem.

I learned from the above experience to inform staff about the purpose of my use of MBWA during the "getting to know you" actions. Since that time, as part of those "getting to know you" meetings, I explained my approach to MBWA. I assured them of my good intentions and did not just walk around. I observed, learned, and very importantly listened (as you get to know staff they will talk and share). I also assured supervisory staff that I would honor the chain of command and as appropriate redirect employees to the proper person in the chain. It has worked well for me. It helps me to have my finger on the pulse so to speak, get to know staff and facilities and programs, and build positive working relationships.

Chapter 4

Communication - Delivering the Message

Communication is a necessary and important part of being a supervisor. It consumes more of the supervisor's time than any other task (you need to communicate in discharging every supervisory task). We probably are communicating even when we are sleeping. The person in bed next to you can hear your bodily noises, any restlessness, and certainly any nightmare related behavior. You may hear or feel yourself at sleep. Have you ever woken up in the morning questioning yourself about a dream or sensing an ache or pain that you did not go to sleep with and wonder what your body is telling you? Have you ever woken up to be questioned by your spouse as to what made you so restless that night or what you were talking about in your sleep? In a way, communication happens 24/7.

Being a good communicator is an important contributor to being a successful supervisor. Being a bad communicator undermines your chances for success. Some say great communicators are born not made. Others insist it can be learned. I am uncertain if either is entirely correct. Ronald Reagan is often called the "Great Communicator." His friend and fellow actor, and politician, also an attorney and political commentator, Senator Fred Thompson said Reagan was the great communicator because he was simple, clear, and sincere in his communications. Was he a born communicator, or was it learned?

I suspect for Reagan it was a combination of nature and learning. Margot Morrell in her book *Reagan's Journey: Lessons of a Remarkable Career* quotes him as saying, in developing a skill "practice, polish, and hone it." Reagan attributes his success to his membership in the Screen Actors Guild of which he eventually became president. He said he learned to communicate attending meetings, listening to others talk, and then synthesizing what they said in formulating his response (good communication is listening and speaking – as you can – think before you speak).

Other great communicators of the current generation and generations past include Queen Elizabeth I, Abe Lincoln, Stephen Douglas, Eleanor Roosevelt, Winston Churchill, Pearl Buck, John Kennedy, Martin Luther King, Bill Clinton, Barack Obama, and Maya Angelou. Can you think of others? In your spare time Google these names and learn more about them and speeches they are remembered for. I confess I know all by name but not nearly everything there is to know about them and what made (makes) them great communicators. I suspect, that like Reagan, their communications were simple, clear, and sincere – good advice for the spoken and written word.

I believe I am a good (even very good) communicator. I've been guided by President Reagan's advice with regards to developing this skill. That is, I practice, polish and hone it constantly.

I was introduced to communication formally for the first time at the age of 12, when I joined the Boy Scouts. I was practicing, polishing and honing communication skills while pursuing such badges as public speaking, citizenship in the community, citizenship in the nation, and citizenship in the world. In elementary and secondary school I learned the rudiments of grammar, spelling, composition and vocabulary. In high school I joined the drama and forensic clubs where I honed those skills more. In college, besides the liberal arts courses, I continued with drama club. In grad school I worked on my writing and presentation skills. My counseling degree was especially useful in learning about active and reflective listening (see Chapter 5). For the past 45 years I've used my communication skills constantly and so have continuously practiced, polished and honed those skills. The skill is not something you learn once and are done. To remain good at the skill you have to use it. As the old saying goes, "use it or lose it."

I've been dying to use a quote on this topic that has become a classic, repeated in many TV shows over the years. The quote, from the 1967 movie *Cool Hand Luke*, goes "What we got here is a failure to communicate." Communication is an important part of each of the chapters in this book. Failure to communicate well can undermine the supervisor's ability to discharge his/ her responsibilities e.g., conflict resolution, decision-making, conducting meetings, and more. It is important that the supervisor choose the most appropriate method to the situation and use that method with skill. The tips that follow the communication methods identified below will assist supervisors in doing so, especially with practice.

Communication Methods

There are a range of communication methods that a supervisor can use. Different methods are more or less suited for the audience, type of message to be communicated, timing, and to some extent, the personal preference of the supervisor. Think of these methods as tools in your communication tool box. There will be times you need to use a hammer, times you will want a screwdriver. Use the best tool for the purpose.

1. **Meetings (Group)** – Meetings are a great way to communicate with your entire team at once, and for that reason, an efficient way, if time and distance allow to get the group together (meetings can be difficult if direct reports span multiple shifts and sites). Face to face communication allows employees to see and hear your delivery, sense your passion and commitment (or lack thereof) to the message (another good reason to practice your remarks). It affords you the opportunity to gauge your audience as you observe how they are reacting as you speak (you might even be able to adjust your message to react to their reactions). It

gives you the opportunity to take and answer questions, clarify your message and prevent misunderstanding in live time. You need to consider a method for getting communications to employees that miss such meetings, especially excused absences, perhaps, a follow-up as in #2 below, minutes of the meeting circulated or posted, or designating co-workers to pass it on (be careful with latter to be sure they are passing on what you said and not what they think you said).

2. **Meetings (one-on-one or in smaller related groups)** – Such meetings could for example be a convening of a smaller group meeting close to the time of a large group meeting to address those staff who could not attend the large group, perhaps because they work a different shift, work a far distance from main location or were otherwise off. Or such meetings can be called to get together a subset of employees about a common project or issue. By experience you will learn that some employees understand better in one-on-one conversations, and so you may intentionally meet that way with some to be sure they understand what was covered in the large group meeting. One-on-one meetings are the preferred method for annual reviews, individual supervision, and discipline (Caution: If one-on-one meetings are generally only used to deal out discipline, that will get out, and when someone is called to the boss' office everyone will assume that person screwed up again. So make sure you use one-on-one meetings for good news too.)

3. **Written** – There are actually a variety of print communication tools that you may use. The two you will most often use are the memo and minutes (of those meetings). The latter serves as documentation of what was said, for future use,

historical record, even evidence, and for the edification of those that miss the meeting. The former is a way to communicate to groups and audiences when convening a meeting is impractical or unnecessary. For example, it would be a waste of time to convene a meeting to announce a new hire or an early dismissal or a (straight-forward) new policy that is pretty straight-forward. Depending on the nature of the work/department you supervise, you may more or less often, want to communicate with fliers, posters and/or brochures. (For help in the development of any of these tools you can find a wealth of direction by Googling each e.g., how to construct an effective memo).

4. **Electronic –**

- Email is the most frequently used form of electronic communication oftentimes preferred over memos. Even when a memo is used, it is often transmitted as an email attachment. It is the one I most use, but not the only one. Remember, different tools serve different purposes. Email is a quick and easy way to reach one or 101 people. You can individually address your emails but you can also create distribution groups making it possible to contact an entire group keying the message just once and hitting the send button. There are a few rules of communication you can use to connote emotion like "yelling in anger" but mostly, email doesn't allow for showing emotions and feelings like you can in meetings. In fact your feelings might be misunderstood in an email, something you might pick up on immediately in a face to face meeting, and therefore adjust for immediately. Emails become permanent records (to a point), that can be helpful later (like when someone says he/she never got the message and you can show it, and perhaps, the receiver's response).

There is a downside. If there is no paper trail and

your computer crashes, it will be difficult, maybe even impossible to recover records. Another disadvantage is that email has become so popular many people find themselves inundated with such messages and so may not open them. They could also inadvertently go into the receiver's spam. While a benefit is the instant delivery of the communication, increasingly such is not really the case. As a time management technique, many people limit their checking email to certain times of the day, some even just once a day. That could leave you assuming someone got a time sensitive message which is sitting in their inbox. And worse yet, have you ever sent an email to the wrong person? Sometimes as you start to key in a name the computer finishes the name for you and if you are not double checking, that might be the wrong name. And, even if you have policies prohibiting sharing or further distribution of an email, an employee might do so intentionally or accidentally.

- Text and instant messages haven't been around as long as email but are increasingly utilized by cell phone users, including supervisors and employees. They are good for short messages and are instant so long as the recipient has his/her device on. Instant messages will only be helpful if all parties have accounts with the same instant messaging service which could have cost implications. IM users have to be signed on to receive messages. Text messages are more likely to be seen sooner than emails and instant messages. Both have pretty much the same positives as email. They are quick, and can be conversational. If there is not unlimited texting in the sender and user's plans, they too can have cost implications. Both are intrusive if the receiver's phone is on and is connected to the IM service. While there is some record of such messages (you can log them), it is harder to organize and retrieve such messages. Texting or instant messaging is especially helpful when you are looking for quick contact and you know the receiver is not near his/her desktop.

- Telephones have come a long way in recent years and seem to be constantly evolving offering employers options for communication. I would guess that most management staff members are less than fully aware of the features of their phone system. Pretty much all have voice messaging, call forwarding, and remote access. Many have conference call capabilities. Some can deliver group messages (e.g., due to the weather there will be a delayed opening till noon today) and schedule meetings.

- Skype, Twitter, and Facebook are what I call emerging tools for supervisor communications. They've been around for about a dozen years, are widely used by the public, and are increasingly being used in business. I confess my relative inexperience as yet in using them as a supervisory tool and so will not cover them in detail. My advice is to acquaint yourself with each as time allows, watch how others use them and as you grow comfortable with them and it seems appropriate, add them to your communication toolbox.

Communication Tips:
Let me share my 12 Step Program for being a good communicator.

1. **Very importantly, use the KISS method. KISS is an acronym for Keep It Simple (or short) Silly (Remember Fred Thompson credited Ronald Reagan as being a good communicator by keeping it simple).** Others have found more colorful words for that second *s*. My undergraduate Essays & Short Stories professor, Fr. Ken O'Leary, when

asked how long our first essay writing assignment should be, said "My dear boy, a good essay is like a mini-skirt; short enough to maintain the reader's interest but long enough to cover the subject."

The KISS method and mini-skirt metaphor are great advice for any spoken or written word. You need to get the message across and not lose the audience's attention. When speaking or writing, remember the old saying "the mind can absorb what the seat can endure." I confess that while I can be short, it is often a challenge. I am constantly reminding myself to be brief and very fortunately, I have trusted family, friends, and peers who know of my penchant to take two or three pages to say what could be said in one page, who are comfortable in reminding me of KISS/mini-skirt. A good general rule of thumb in writing memos is to keep the message to one page. Emails too should be short (with all the emails people get, they are more likely to read one with a clear subject line and one that is short). Here is where the practice and polish come in. I write my memo draft, print it out to see how long it is (if you are technologically savvy enough you can just put your software in page layout view. When I see how long or short it is I can add more or delete accordingly (most often I do more deleting than adding, and sometimes delete one thing so I can add another).

2. **If you have something important to say, say it again and again.** Winston Churchill stressed this tip when speaking to students at his alma mater the Harrow School (10/29/1941) when he said "– If you have an important point to make, don't try to be subtle or clever. Use a pile driver. Hit the point once. Then come back and hit it again. Then hit it a third time – a tremendous whack." There is actually research (Pilcher, September 23, 2014, *The Financial Brand*)

which confirms that messages are more effective when repeated. Repeating a message better assures that it is heard and remembered. I recommend too, that in repeating your message, you mix it up. Use different mediums, perhaps in a speech, in a memo and an email, and maybe paraphrased in one-on-one or smaller group conversations and discussions. As I just said repetition better assures the message was heard. It also generally leads the recipient/audience to understand it is important. Mixing it up helps in two ways. Some people receive messages better in different forms, e.g., memo, email or spoken word. Repeating the message exactly the same way whether in the same or different forms can start to annoy; mixing it up creates the repetition effect without becoming annoying. There is actually a time when repetition, regardless of how the message is delivered, becomes annoying. I honestly do not think there is a magic number. I feel safe in saying it is o.k. to deliver the message three or four times to the same audience without such a risk. Beyond that I would suggest that before repeating it a fifth or more time, you allow a break period, perhaps weeks or a month if time will allow, or seek feedback from trusted staff about whether or not repeating it will turn the recipients off to the message.

I think the majority of authors writing on this matter (repeating the message several times) would agree with Churchill and me, that it is not only o.k. but wise to do so. Some would disagree with me. Recently I read an article on communication that advised against repetition. The reason given was that it might bore the audience or be perceived as insulting. I think the benefit of assuring the message is heard outweighs that concern. Seeking employee feedback on the frequency of communications in general, and on the repetition of individual messages will assist the supervisor in making such communication decisions.

3. **The bell cannot be unrung.** Never respond to an email, or an event, that occurs while you are angry. Even if you recall an email message, it is unlikely you will prevent its being read. Those communications can start an email war exchange, damage work relations and cause a toxic work environment. I generally do one of two things. I might draft an email response but hold sending it or send it to myself, allowing time to cool off and think a bit more rationally, and/or seek feedback from a trusted person. I prefer the sending to myself option because preparing a response with an email address in the "to" box might lead to an accidental sending. I can almost guarantee sending an email while angry or upset, will lead to regret or worse. Don't act in haste. If possible, sleep on it; wait a few hours; wait at least an hour.

4. **Again, the bell cannot be unrung. I offer the same advice before responding in memo form or orally.** Things said or written in anger often come back to bite you. Please do not construe my advice to mean to ignore such communications. Ignoring them too can be problematic, like letting a wound fester rather than clean and treat it. Respond, but do so from a position of calm and reasoned thought.

5. **If you use email instead of old fashioned memo or letter, I recommend two things.** Check with your employer to confirm if your emails are backed up on a server someplace that can be retrieved if your computer crashes. Even if you have such an assurance, you may find it difficult to retrieve messages in the timeframe you need them, so selectively keep hard copies of sent and received messages.

6. **When using email consider time saving and effectiveness steps like using a boiler plate form for messages with**

organization name and contact information, your own printed name and contact information, and perhaps, signature. A great deal of time can be saved using such a format, rather than constantly keying in that information on each separate email (you can even have different boiler plate formats for different purposes). Consider including organization Mission Statement on these forms.

7. **When you have a choice and know the receiver's preferred communication mode, use it.** In my last position, one of my direct reports preferred text messages over email. How did I know this was important to her? Because she told me, and told me, and told me, sometimes in person, sometimes by email. In fact I avoided texting in general, until in responding to her request to use texting, I became comfortable texting her, and others.

8. **Become familiar with the phone system at your organization.** There are often short manuals, even one page laminated cheat sheets given to users. Read them and use the features that can help you. Ask for the full manual. Ask perhaps for a formal training for you and staff. Google the name of your system online for more information.

9. **In your written communications, e.g., emails and memos write something in the subject line.** Keep the title short so the audience knows what it is about and you get their attention, increasing the chance the recipient will read it. Leaving the subject line blank might cause your email to end up in the recipient's spam mail/junk box. Check correspondence for grammar and spelling. If it is available, use spell-check. Beware of the auto-correct function. Always proofread carefully. Sometimes auto-correct can have you saying something you did not want to say. Have

someone you trust review messages going out to large groups (and certainly to those above you in the chain of command). Be careful when using Siri (or similar dictation software) when texting. This could lead to embarrassment in any situation but can be more problematic when it is a work related message.

10. **Practice what you say – literally.** Some people are good at speaking extemporaneously (off the top of their head) on a range of topics. Most are not. Speaking unprepared leads to wandering off topic, hesitation, and the dreaded words "ah, like, and you know" often turning your audience off. I recommend writing down what you want to say, word for word or in some sort of outline. I recommend it for formal planned remarks such as at a staff meeting but even for planned informal discussions with individual staff. It helps organize your thoughts and better assures you say what you want to say (sometimes you have to wing it but when you don't have to, don't). After you organize those thoughts and pen them down, practice them. Sometimes I look in the mirror at home, even in the bathroom at work so I can see my facial expressions and body movements (and practice them). I go so far in practicing to stand at a podium or sit to replicate how I will present to the audience. Occasionally I have a trusted staff or family member listen and watch and give me feedback. I regularly use driving time to prepare and practice remarks. Oftentimes, when planning a one-on-one or group meeting where I expect there to be a give and take I consider possible audience comments, questions and reactions and practice possible responses (always guided by that Boy Scout Motto).

11. **Never say "I am only going to say this once..** Making such a statement before delivering a message would indicate

what is about to be said is important. But what happens if you say it once and come to believe it was not heard as widely as you expected? Very likely, you will say it again. In doing so you are sending a message that you don't always mean what you say. That could lead employees not to listen as closely to your messages because they will assume you will repeat it later anyway. Further, employees may generalize and start questioning if you mean other things you say.

12. **A good ground rule for meetings whether individual or group would be to have cell phones off.** Any audible noise will can distract the speaker and the audience, sometimes causing the speaker to lose his/her train of thought. Some people put their phones on vibrate but that sensation can distract the receiver of the message too. Another is to start and end on time even if all do not show on time (they will learn). Consider having a written agenda for meetings, circulated in advance and allow staff to suggest agenda items before the agenda is finalized. Agendas can help keep meetings more orderly and focused. Consider circulating minutes of meetings as a reminder, a record, even evidence.

Case Examples

"What we got here is a failure to Communicate." When I assumed the position of president of Catholic Charities, I would often send board members informational packets (trees died). This was in the late 90s and most communicating was sent by US mail. At a board meeting I asked of the board if they had gotten the last packet I sent them. Mostly heads were nodding indicating yes. One brave soul volunteered he had received it and the many others I sent and he was drowning in information, would not read it all and pleaded with me to stop.

Seventeen years later at a meeting of the same board I placed on the agenda a discussion of the frequency of board meetings. We had been meeting ten times a year. I was suggesting we meet quarterly. The board unanimously approved the change. One board member said my emails to them each month kept them fully informed such that he was very comfortable meeting less often. He said those reports were short, timely and informative. Other board members echoed his comments.

I learned a lesson from the "drowning in information" incident. I was overwhelming some board members (probably most, maybe even all) with information to the point they were only selectively reading and missing some important information (what we got here is a failure to communicate – effectively). Communication as handled in the 17 years later incident consisted of a once a month summary email report to the board that highlighted one important fact or occurrence in each department distilled from each department head report to me of two or three one liners. In addition I would email board members once or twice a week with short informational messages of occurrences of note (good and not so good). I learned over the years to communicate effectively and in as few words as possible, applying the learning and practicing the communication tips cited above.

Chapter 5

Communication – Receiving the Message

What is Active Listening?

Have you ever played the party game "telephone"? Growing up it was right up there with postman and spin the bottle at birthday parties. Googling the title in preparing this chapter, I was surprised to learn that it is still a popular game today for children and adults. It is frequently used as an ice breaker for workshops and presentations on communication. I've used this game as an ice breaker in training my staff in the technique of active listening. Telephone is a good and fun way of demonstrating the importance of listening to effective verbal communication. For the full rules of play, instructions, even sample words or phrases to use, Google "the game telephone." Maybe you'll use it with your staff. In brief, players stand in a line or sit in a circle or around a table. The messenger (frequently the party boy or girl) starts by whispering a message in the ear of the person next to him/her. That message can be one word but if so, should be multisyllabic and unusual, or, a phrase that is alliterative and not a familiar phrase like "Peter picked a peck of pickled peppers." It is passed from person to person. If a person asks to repeat the message, don't. The initial messenger should write the message on a piece of paper before delivering it the first time. When the last person receives the message, he/she says it out loud. Most often, the final message is nothing like the first. Discussing how the message was changed in transmission makes the case for active listening. To make the case for active listening training, play the game a second time with this rule change. As each person receives the message he/she can ask the messenger to repeat the message. Then the receiver says "Did I hear you right, you said... " (fill in this blank). The accuracy of transmission greatly increases.

This game/exercise, demonstrates the importance of active listening to good verbal communication. Verbal communication has two components, content (the facts and words), and feeling, which requires the development of active listening skills. Good communication requires the use of mouth, eyes and ears. Some say having two ears but only one mouth indicates a good communicator should listen twice as much as he/she talks. My point is to be a good communicator you need to be good at talking (delivering a message) and at listening (able to accurately hear others' messages). Seeing the delivery of the message contributes to accurately receiving the full message. The good listener uses his/her eyes and ears to observe body language and hear or sense the feeling or emotion being communicated, then reflects the message back to the presenter, both content and feeling, who will confirm or correct the message. Sometimes body language communicates something different from what is said. Have you ever been in a conversation where someone is giving you instructions and at the end asks if you understand; embarrassed to say that you don't, you say "Yes" only to have the person say, "Are you sure, you look a bit confused?" The initiator read your body language, that facial expression that contradicted your "yes" which would lead to a restatement or clarification of the original message resulting in more clarity and understanding and you being able to follow those instructions.

Active Listening is Important to Good Communication

Active listening builds positive relationships with and among staff, clients/customers and vendors; leads to understanding, prevents and solves conflict, leads to problem-solving, improves accuracy while reducing errors, and increases productivity, effectiveness and profits.

Listening helps assure you hear the message accurately and get the facts. Such information will assure you carry out directions or have the necessary information to make decisions or take action. Suppose your boss gives you instructions about a meeting, what it is about, day, time and location. Suppose part of that communication was it would be next Wednesday (and it is Monday now). Are you clear on the meeting being in two days hence or is it the next Wednesday after this one? You might miss or be late for an important meeting and if you are passing the message on to others you might have an unhappy boss. Asking the boss to confirm which Wednesday will clarify the communication, save wasted time and save embarrassment.

Listening to a job applicant's responses to your job interview questions will help answer questions you might have about the paperwork before you (the application and resume). Hearing the excitement in the applicant's voice and seeing it in his/her face as you discuss the organization's Mission will help you decide whether the candidate is a good fit for the organization. Conversely, detecting in the applicant's body language a lack of support or enthusiasm for the Mission might be a good reason not to offer the job to an otherwise qualified applicant.

Listening builds trust. Using the meeting scheduling example above, had the employee persisted in saying he understood and then missed the meeting, that would likely undermine the supervisor's trust in future communications with the employee. As the example played out, trust gets built in two ways. The employee receiving the initial message learns it is okay to say I'm not sure and ask for clarification and builds trust. The supervisor trusts that when his/her instructions aren't clear, that the employee will ask and so builds trust that way.

Listening can prevent or reduce conflict. One source of conflict occurs when someone feels misunderstood or mistreated. If the person delivering that message is unaware you misunderstood the communication that can become a festering wound, poisoning the work relationship between the two of you and even creating a toxic work environment. It is in situations such as this when you observe facial expressions, gestures, or other behaviors that contradict the words, you should ask questions and in so doing, prevent future problems. Good listening skills not only prevent misunderstandings among your employees, it prevents misunderstandings with clients/customers, helping to make good first impressions with them, and enhances the organization's reputation (and satisfied customers tell others, which again is good for your reputation and for business). Listening helps motivate employees and builds a positive work environment.

Being a good listener will help you improve morale and productivity. The better a supervisor listens to employees, the better he/she understands and knows them, their likes and dislikes, their strengths and weaknesses. The easier it is to address those things, the easier it is to motivate them. As you get to know your employees better, it will help you to better choose appropriate rewards from those available to you, adding to their job satisfaction, maintaining and improving morale. Giving basketball tickets e.g., as a reward to someone who doesn't like basketball, is not so rewarding.

Active Listening – A 12 Step Program

1. **When you can, choose the place and time to minimize distractions and interruptions and assure privacy.** It demonstrates respect for the person and helps create an environment conducive to good communication. Control for people and phone interruptions, background noise such as music or loud machinery (turn off cell phones or put on silent, close windows, shut doors, move away from the desk where the phone could be ignored more easily). When I met with someone in my office, unless I wanted to impress upon the person that I was the boss and power person in the relationship, I left my desk with the phone and papers and moved to my conference table,

always sitting across from the person, never sitting at the head of the table. I closed the door to better assure privacy and confidentiality and discourage interruptions. If the place chooses you like in the middle of the work area, something happens that requires communication, or someone else is the initiator of the conversation you can suggest/request moving the conversation elsewhere. This too shows respect for the other party and leads to more accurate communication.

2. **Face the other party or parties and maintain eye contact and keep a comfortable distance.** Distance is pretty much determined by the size of the table if you are sitting at a table for a conversation. Even with a table there is a choice where to sit. Don't take a seat at the other end of the table from the other person(s). Sit in close proximity to the other party(ies) (in US culture two feet is generally a good distance but be aware that different cultures have different norms). If you're having a standing conversation and you are too close or far away from the other party, you will likely find he/she will step closer or move farther away and you will observe by their body language that they become more comfortable with the adjusted difference. If the conversation is taking place seated, similarly you may find the person moving the chair closer or further for the same reason (or to hear you better). Face the person you are speaking to and maintain eye contact. It conveys respect, and helps both parties to be more attentive, assuring more effective communication. If two or more persons are party to the conversation, look the person in the eye who you are talking to or listening to; if addressing more than one person at a time, shift eye contact among the listeners (especially when addressing a large audience).

3. **Be and remain attentive and relaxed.** If you can, before you start the meeting give thought to what you want to say, and how, even possible comments and questions the listener might make, take a deep cleansing breath or two, and clear your mind of distractions. Throughout the conversation maintain the eye contact mentioned in Step 2 but avoid staring and watch out for letting your own thoughts and feelings run through your mind while listening. Sit comfortably in the chair but lean forward a bit. It will help you focus on the person speaking and lets the speaker know he/she has your attention. Keep both feet on the ground and do not cross your legs if you are a male, and do not lean back in the chair as these behaviors convey just the opposite.

4. **Be and remain open minded.** This can be challenging. In the helping field this step might be titled "suspend judgment." The person may say something that you think is stupid or silly, and/or be of concern. Your mind could easily start judging the person, leading you to draw early and possibly wrong conclusions, causing you to miss important facts and feelings. You might be tempted to interrupt the speaker, finishing his/her sentence, thinking you know where the conversation is going. If you were wrong in your assumption, you may never know, as the other person will draw his or her own conclusions, like you don't care or understand, and clam up. I learned from experience that staff, clients, and customers will say some strange even bizarre things leading you to tune them out and in so doing shut them down and miss something important. If something is important and you are being attentive, the speaker will say it two, even three times. But if the speaker feels you are not listening, he will shut down. One of my first bosses was fond of telling me and

other staff "there is no such thing as a stupid question, so do not be afraid to ask." That helped create an atmosphere where I felt comfortable asking questions when I did not know or was not sure, and as a result, communication was much better. Similarly if you think something the speaker says is stupid or wrong, even if you do not come out and say it, you may show your disapproval in other ways, so avoid judging.

5. **A picture is worth a thousand words.** You won't remember every word that is said. So try to paint a mental picture; try to envision the words and feelings being communicated concentrating on and trying to remember key words, phrases, sentences and feelings expressed or sensed, and body language observed. This will help you better retain the speaker's content information and accompanying feelings. Keep writing to a minimum but have paper and pen to jot down key words, statements, feelings sensed or expressed, to help your recall later.

6. **Avoid interrupting and don't suggest solutions.** Are you of an age to remember the T.V. show "Father Knows Best" (vintage 1950s)? The characters always came to the father (Jim Anderson, played by Robert Young) with their problems, not looking for help in deciding what to do, but looking for father who knows best to tell them what to do. While some folks may want you to tell them what to do, doing that does not help them develop the problem-solving and decision-making skills needed to succeed. Most people don't want you to give them the answer. They want you to help them figure out the answer. When listening to someone talk about a problem, you may be tempted to interrupt, say you understand exactly what the problem is and say you know exactly what to do. You

may even stop listening because you are planning your response in your mind, meanwhile missing something that could be important. When you interrupt you may cause the speaker to lose his or her train of thought; imply you don't care what they have to say or that it is unimportant; or suggest that you know better than them, that you know what is best. That could sabotage trust in the work relationship, and lead to conflict and a dysfunctional work environment.

7. **Wait for a pause in the conversation to ask a clarifying question.** As you listen, there will be things that aren't clear or about which you have a question. Try not to interrupt (for the reasons cited in #6 above). Hold your thought until the speaker pauses. If need be, jot down a word or two to remind yourself what you wish to question. When there is a pause or the speaker stops then ask the clarifying question "Can you repeat what you said when you said…, I want to be sure I heard you right," or, "Can you tell me what you meant (and/or what you felt) when you said…" This allows the speaker to finish uninterrupted and demonstrates respect for the speaker, and in asking the question confirms you have been listening while getting you that clarifying information.

8. **Ask questions relevant to the purpose of the conversation.** Keep in mind the advice already given above about not interrupting. An easy way to interrupt not only the speaker's words, but his/her thoughts, is to ask questions unrelated to the topic of discussion. For example, an employee may be reporting to you what was covered at a meeting you asked him/to attend. While reporting on the meeting the speaker might mention he/she ran into a person who said he knew you. You might remark you

haven't seen him in years and ask one or more questions about him causing the speaker to move off subject. The speaker may be distracted from the intended message, and could easily run out of time. Not that I would encourage doing this intentionally but do you ever recall yourself or perhaps a classmate purposely asking a question off topic to waste time (like when you were expecting a pop quiz to be announced)? If you notice your question has the conversation moving off topic, redirect it. In the above example you could interrupt and say it was nice to hear from so and so, maybe you could tell me more about what he said later, but I don't want to short change you so let's hear more about the meeting.

9. **Demonstrate empathy for the speaker.** I remember the first time I heard the word empathy. It was over forty years ago in my undergraduate educational psychology class. The professor introduced the concept by telling the class this old Cherokee proverb "Don't judge a man until you have walked a mile in his moccasins (shoes)." American author Nelle Harper Lee in her book *To Kill a Mockingbird* may have been influenced by this proverb when she wrote "You never really know a man until you understand things from his point of view, until you climb into his skin and walk around in it."

You need to put yourself in the speaker's place and imagine what it is like for the speaker at the moment (view the situation from the speaker's perspective). It is generally hard to do especially if you don't have that shared experience. Suppose for example you are terminating an employee and you have never experienced being terminated yourself. As the soon-to-be former employee responds to the news, he/she likely will have and express strong feelings, like surprise, anger, fear.

Even if you had the experience of being fired you cannot be certain which feelings this person will have, nor the strength of the feelings. But you can draw upon your own and others' experiences of loss, of receiving bad, life changing news that might help you. The important thing is to be aware of your own feelings as the conversation unfolds, try to avoid transferring your feelings to the speaker, and very importantly, keep asking yourself what the speaker is feeling as he/she hears the news. Try to understand the motivation behind the speaker's feelings. Feelings of fear may be motivated by concerns of bills to be paid, loss of housing, inability to provide for family. Knowing, for example, that there is a sick child at home will certainly help you understand feelings of anger and fear in the employee.

10. **Reflect the speaker's content and feeling while trying to avoid interrupting.** Have you ever been on the phone listening to someone and that person says "Are you still there?" In your effort to listen you are so quiet, the speaker may think you were cut off. Not only do you want to show the speaker you are listening; you also want to check in with the speaker to affirm that you are listening and that you are hearing the message accurately. A great vocabulary for conveying that you are paying attention without interrupting the speaker and his/her train of thought would include words or expressions such as "Uh huh, I see, and?, hmm, yes, oh?, go on, tell me more." Your body language too can convey you are listening and that you understand. A smile on your face when the speaker is telling you some really good news e.g., about the birth of a child, conveys you know the speaker is experiencing joy. A sad face when the speaker is describing a sad event conveys you understand he is sad. Occasionally use whole

sentences to confirm the message and encourage the speaker to continue. Saying "That must have been very hard for you to say" confirms you heard the message and if you didn't, gives the speaker the opportunity to straighten you out. Comments like "It sounds like you were confused" or "You must have been overjoyed when… " also are minimally interruptive while allowing the speaker to confirm and or correct your understanding.

As needed to clarify remarks or fill in blanks, ask questions, but sparingly. If you can wait till there is a pause in the conversation, do so. Or, you can wait for the conversation to change direction. For purposes of encouraging further communication use open ended versus closed ended questions (the former to be answered in sentences, the latter a short yes or no). For example if the speaker is telling you a co-worker isn't carrying her weight and you are uncertain how she feels about it, rather than use a closed ended question such as "Are you surprised by so and so's performance?" you might ask her "How do you feel about so and so not carrying her weight?" The closed ended question gets a short answer that may necessitate follow-up questions to get more information. The short answer may give you only the partial truth. In the above example the employee may say yes she was surprised and the conversation stops there. But in answering the open ended question more useful information might be shared such as she was surprised, hurt that someone she thought was a friend might be dumping on her and co-workers who pick up the slack, angry over the situation or sad because now she is losing a friend.

11. **Watch body language, yours and theirs.** When listening, remember to listen for content and for feeling. Lots of times, especially until a trust relationship has been built between

the parties, the speaker may tend to hide or understate their emotions and feelings. Look for facial expressions and other body language, keeping in mind that words are only a portion of the message. The speed with which the speaker talks, the fire in the belly, tone of voice, look on his/her face, clenching of fists, sitting on edge of seat are also part of the communication of the message which you need to confirm and clarify as mentioned in Step 10 above.

Be aware that you can send negative messages via your own body language. Breaking eye contact, crossing of your arms, sitting back in your chair as opposed to feet on ground and leaning forward, tapping your feet, shaking head (like no) as the speaker converses, can be an indication to him/her that you disagree, disapprove or dislike what is being said, or that you are just not interested. Doing so may cause the speaker to stop sharing then and in the future. So suspend judgment in what you say and don't say.

12. **Practice, Practice, Practice.** Have you ever heard the Carnegie Hall joke? Tourist in NYC goes up to a stranger and asks "How do you get to Carnegie Hall?" The stranger responds "Practice." Many believe the origin of that joke involves famed violinist Mischa Elman who when asked how he got to Carnegie Hall said "Practice." The point of the joke is that practice is needed to be a good communicator. Practice may not make you perfect but it will make you a good communicator. And continued practice will keep you good and make you better.

Try this simple exercise to get started. At home with your spouse or significant other, and/or at work with a trusted co-worker, at the end of a conversation briefly summarize what you heard or what you believe you said. When the other party says "Heh, I just said that" you will know you are on to something. As you progress, you will get better at summarizing the content and adding in the feelings expressed too.

Here is another exercise you can try to test the validity about the proper distance between the conversing parties that I mentioned in Step 2 above. When standing for a conversation with a co-worker, after a few seconds, start to inch closer. Very likely as you continue to inch closer, you will notice the other party inching away as you violate his personal space. Or do the opposite and inch away and note the other party inching closer. Besides doing this for the fun of the exercise, remain aware of it and make those adjustments in your conversations for the comfort of the person you are speaking to.

Read and re-read the 12 Steps and practice them in real life conversations, or if you have a willing partner, in simulated conversations. As you continue to practice, you will get better at communicating and feel better as you do. And as you get better at listening, the majority of those you speak to will be more comfortable speaking and revealing to you. A more positive work environment will result.

Case Example of Poor Active Listening Skills Leading to Conflict

It was over forty years ago. I had my first supervisory job. Over a period of time I noticed a change in a particular employee with whom I had a good and friendly working relationship. His body language started to convey impatience when I spoke to him or gave him direction. He just looked unhappy. He would avoid conversations with me even leave the room (if he could) when I entered. Other employees asked me what was wrong between the two of us. I finally called a private meeting, told him I sensed there was a growing problem and asked if there was anything wrong. He identified a meeting over six months ago in which I made a comment that was personally offensive to him. At the time I did not even recall the meeting or the comment. I apologized for offending him and assured him I held him in high regard and valued his work. We agreed we would move forward. Unfortunately he did not move forward or put the matter behind. His job performance dropped off and he started to become publicly insubordinate, ultimately leading to his termination. I sometimes wonder had I picked up on his body language sooner or had he trusted me enough to confront me with his concerns, if the conflict and termination could have been avoided. I believe if I had the active listening skills I have today, back then, things would have been different.

Chapter 6

Conflict Management

Death, Taxes and Conflict

Benjamin Franklin once said "In this world nothing can be said to be certain, except death and taxes" (*The Works of Benjamin Franklin, 1817*). Conflict too is a certainty. It is a fact of life, a fact of work life. It is not a matter of will there be conflict in the workplace; it's a matter of when. It's a matter to be managed. When two or more people work together, there will be conflict. US workers spend almost three hours each week dealing with conflict (CPP Human Capital Report, July, 2008, page 3).

Check Your Attitude.

Fr. Joseph Martin a pioneer in the field of alcoholism treatment describes attitudes as the father of the action (*Fr. Martin's Guidelines for Alcoholics*, part 1, 1976). He illustrates that statement with this story:

> A man walks into a psychiatrist's office and says to the doctor "Doc, you have to help me, I'm dead." The doctor took the man into an exam room, checked his vital signs [all normal] explained that dead people don't have a heart-beat, don't breathe and do not have a blood pressure reading. He spent a good hour with the man but could not convince him that he was alive. The doctor was intrigued and came up with a plan. He told the man he could cure him of his problem in thirty days. He told him that for the next thirty days he was to look in a mirror three times a day and say to himself "Dead people do not bleed" and come back to see him after that. The man returned on day 31. The doctor took him into an exam room, sat him down, and pricked his finger. The man bled, his jaw

dropped, there was a look of surprise on his face. The smart doctor was so proud anticipating the man's acknowledgment that he was alive when the man burst out "Good heavens doc, dead people do bleed."

The point of his story is that our attitudes control our actions (as he says it "our attitudes are the father of the action"), and they are hard to change. Fr. Martin uses this story to introduce his audience to the possibility of helping alcoholics by first challenging the audience to examine their attitude towards alcoholism and alcoholics. He points out that our attitudes which affect what we believe and what we think about things, are formed from a very early age, and reinforced as we grow up, and so are difficult to change or overcome (but not impossible).

Boris Karloff playing Frankenstein (*The Bride of Frankenstein* 1935) tenses up and says "Fire no good [bad]" as the blind man who befriends him lights a cigar. In the first movie *Frankenstein*, he learned fire was bad when his creator's henchman used a torch to control him. It was with difficulty that the blind man convinced Frankenstein that fire was good.

We all have an attitude about conflict. It was learned when we were young, reinforced at home, school, and work. Expressions like "Children should be seen and not heard", "Because I said so (parent and boss)", "Don't rock the boat", "Everyone should just get along", "Don't talk back", "Don't disrespect your elders (or the boss)" and the accompanying reinforcing behaviors go a long way towards explaining the attitude of those that avoid or discourage conflict. Some learned a different attitude about conflict, winning at all costs. The kid who has to be the best at everything, very likely grows up having to be the best at work too, placing stress on self, others, and the work environment. Work is not a sporting event where there are winners and losers, it is a team event. If you cause a fellow team member to lose, eventually you will pay the price e.g., when you need his or his co-workers' help and you don't get it. Examine your attitude towards conflict and be open to changing it. Attitudes can be changed. It will likely take some time. Start today!

Conflict: Good or Bad?

Here's a thought. Conflict, well managed, is the supervisor's friend. Conflict, poorly managed or ignored, is bad. Managing conflict is a part of every supervisor's job. It is a learned behavior. If you want to be a good supervisor you will need to manage conflict. So accept it, embrace it, manage it. Friedrich Nietzsche said "That which does not kill us, makes us stronger" (*Twilight of the Idols*, 1888). If conflict is well managed, the work environment will be strengthened; productivity will improve; the team will be strengthened; better and new solutions will be found; staff will grow, the department will be stronger. If conflict is not well managed, the work place will become toxic (maybe even die). Conflict should be expected, anticipated, and dealt with positively, respectfully and timely.

Types of Conflict

Jean Lebedun (1998, page 27) identifies four types of conflict:

1. Conflict over facts or data
2. Conflict over process or methods
3. Conflict over purpose
4. Conflict over Values

It is helpful to know what type of conflict you are facing. Some types are more difficult than others. Knowing what type you are dealing with makes it easier to identify the cause(s) and better plan for addressing and resolving the conflict.

1. Conflict over facts or data

If the different sides are relying on different facts or data or different sources of information, there will likely be differences in understanding and differences of opinion leading to conflict. Both sides might be relying on the law in drawing a conclusion but perhaps one is relying on a federal statute and the other is relying on a comparable state statute, or an earlier un-amended version. Each side might be relying on a different expert's report. Clarifying what each other's source of the facts is and what those facts are, often quickly lead to agreement on those facts and speedy amicable solution.

2. **Conflict over process or methods**

   A clash over the best way to accomplish a goal or assignment is the most common source of workplace conflict (Lebedun, 1998). Consider this example. The boss says the budget needs to be reduced by ten percent. You convene a staff meeting to settle upon the approach. Some might say simply cut every budget item by ten percent. Some will favor cutting one or more budget lines entirely (training and travel are often the first on the chopping block). There will likely be a range of recommended line items to be cut. Some might suggest renegotiating contracts. Some might offer revenue generating ideas. Comparing the pros and cons of each method can lead to better understanding, agreement on one or more combination of methods, and possibly, even on a new method.

3. **Conflict over purpose.**

   Have you ever heard one employee saying to another "Why are we doing this anyway?" While two or more people may be working on the same project they could be doing it for different reasons which could affect levels of commitment and decision-making along the way. It helps when people come together to work on an issue or project, that there be a sharing among the participants of what each person's purpose is for doing so.

4. Conflict over Values

This type of conflict is the most difficult to deal with. Values guide actions. They're ingrained in us, not easily turned on or off. Values aren't something you want folks to turn on and off for different situations. You want people to be true to their values. It is helpful in such situations that the parties know what each others' values are and what the organization's values are. In these types of conflicts, there can be understanding of all the values involved yet have disagreement on the solution in which case the course of action may be decided by an arbitrator or you. If a person's values are inconsistent with the organization's values, that person might want to consider working elsewhere where he/she can enjoy more job satisfaction.

12 Step Conflict Management Program

1. **Before conflict occurs heed the message of Chapter 1.** *You are now forewarned that conflict is a fact of work-life, so be forearmed and "Be Prepared."* Be certain you understand the Organization's Sacred Documents, most especially the Mission Statement. Be certain you know the Main Thing for your department. Then be certain your staff is aware of them and that everyone commits to them. If people are aware of these documents, understand they are important, when conflict arises these documents can be the yardstick against which to test possible solutions. Asking the question "Does this option support the Mission and Main Thing?" will help to focus discussion on what is best for the department rather than for any one individual.

2. **Before conflict occurs develop and practice good communication skills for yourself and help staff to do the same (Chapters 5 & 6).** Communication is a frequent cause of conflict (Myatt, page 2). Clear communications will go a long way towards preventing conflict and towards resolving it when it does occur. If communication is poor, efforts to resolve conflict might worsen it.

3. **Before conflict occurs be working on developing and maintaining a Positive Work Environment (Chapter 13).** If there is a positive work environment employees will be more likely to feel safe to tell you about brewing conflicts, and more importantly, tell the other party(ies) to it, and resolve it on their own, or ask for help.

4. **Before conflict occurs get to know your employees and have them get to know each other (Chapter 15).** As you know someone better, you can sense when something is off, be alert to flashpoints before there is a blowout (*CPP Global Human Capital Report*, 2008, pages 11 & 14). You and they can choose more appropriate communication techniques for the person on the receiving end of the communication, which will help prevent conflict and resolve it more easily and quickly when it occurs.

5. **Before conflict occurs develop your own and staff's decision-making skills.** They will be useful in deciding if and when to intervene in a conflict situation and aide in selecting the best solution among alternatives identified.

6. **Before conflict occurs create and maintain a Dynamic Learning Environment (Chapter 12).** Less than half the employers in the US provide conflict management training

for staff (*CPP Global Human Capital Report*, 2008, page 3). Don't be one of them. The same report found that the "most common denominator to successful conflict resolution is formal training" (*CPP Global Human Capital Report*, 2008, page 3). And offer conflict management training (and not just one-time). Offer training on related topics, including but not limited to Mission, communication, listening, and decision-making.

7. **When conflict occurs set ground rules for dealing with the matter.** Don't take for granted that everyone knows what they are. Be specific e.g., start and end sessions on time, no yelling, no personal attacks, certainly no physical attacks, one person talks at a time, agree to listen to others. I advise asking the participants for additional suggestions. I advise giving each participant a copy of the ground rules and ask them to bring them to meetings.

8. **Share your understanding of the issues, the facts in the case as you understand them, why the matter is important to you and the organization, what the differences are, what emotions and feelings seem to be involved (yours and others), and what you need to have happen.** Ask the participant(s) to reflect back what they heard you say (active listening). Then ask each participant to share their understanding of the issues in the same way you just did after which you reflect what you heard and if there are more than the two of you ask the others to add anything they heard. Obtain agreement from the participants on a summary of the discussion (keep and share that summary for record/evidence, and follow-up).

9. **Brainstorm a list of possible approaches or solutions (on the spirit of brainstorming from the decision-making**

chapter). At this point the effort is for volume and not evaluating or judging.

10. **Evaluate the brainstorming list identifying pros and cons of each considering the impact of each on the department/ organization, the Mission and Main Thing and fellow employees.** If time is needed to further evaluate one or more items on the list, assign any homework and schedule a follow-up session.

11. **Ask the group which items on the brainstorming list are most promising.** Perhaps one or two surface as clear best choice(s). Discuss further scheduling another meeting if it appears allowing more time for further consideration or reflection would be useful. After that, by consensus if it exists or fiat if it does not, announce the solution, explain the reasoning and inform audience and others that would need to know and then implement.

12. **Evaluate.** Monitor the work environment to assess the effectiveness of the solution. You may find all is fine. You may find there is still underlying or residual conflict (especially hurt feelings) that should be addressed. Sometimes, in solving one matter, the solution might spawn a new one, so be attentive. This step might just include an audience of one (you). But I recommend that at the end of Step 11 you announce a time (perhaps two or three weeks hence) to come back together as a group to jointly assess progress.

One Size Does Not Fit All

I believe that following the 12 Step Program above will prove effective in managing conflict. But it is not the only way. I suggest you be guided by it, use it or parts of it that work for you, and or, adapt it for use all the time or for different situations. There may be times when the issue is of such importance to you, your boss, and/or to the organization, that you may feel it necessary to simply say "This is the way it is going down." Even then I recommend explaining your reasoning and ongoing monitoring for any untoward consequences.

I like to modify the 12 Steps, taking myself out of it initially and allowing the conflicting parties to work the Steps on their own (very empowering). I was influenced in developing this approach from training I took with Richard Lazar, PhD in the late 1970s (LazarAchievementPsychology.com). Dr. Lazar provided extensive management training at St. Joseph's Hospital where I worked at the time. In covering conflict management he provided us training in the use of the win-win approach. My modified approach presumes that some work has already been done on Steps 1 -6 above. I invite staff that has a conflict to approach the person or persons they have the conflict with, follow the 12 Step Program and try to work it out between themselves. At the same time, all the employees know that at any time in the process, if one or both (all) parties feel they need help they state so and bring the matter to my attention. In the Lazar training we learned to use a trigger phrase to get the other party's attention. The phrase he introduced was "I have a disturbance." Anytime someone said that to another person it was expected that person would listen and agree to a quick time to meet to discuss and attempt to resolve the conflict. In practice in recent years I directed staff to use as a trigger phrase "I have a problem." For more information on Dr. Lazar's approach to conflict management visit http:// lazarachievementpsychology.com/ebook.

Sometimes I prefer to use a mediator reasoning I need help on this one, or perhaps, they might respond better with a neutral third party facilitator. Over the years I have on rare occasion paid an external mediator. Such a decision could be beyond your authority or budget. If so your HR department might provide this function or there could be some other respected supervisor in the organization that you might ask.

Conflict Re-defined: $A + B = C$

A. Conflict, well managed, leads to better understanding of issues and challenges. It leads to a better understanding of the pluses and minuses to the alternatives under consideration. It can lead to a peaceful solution to the matter, sometimes to an entirely new and better solution that would not have been considered absent the conflict.

B. Conflict, well managed, leads to better understanding among those involved, of each other's needs, ideas, ways of thinking, communication styles, and beliefs. It builds trust among those involved strengthening work relationships and making it easier to work together moving forward.

C. A + B results in increased productivity, innovation, improved morale, increased cooperation and better. It helps build a positive (more positive) stronger work environment where employees feel safe and comfortable in speaking their minds and suggesting a different way or approach which almost always yields better decisions, and sometimes, even a breakthrough innovation.

Conclusion

The 12 Step program described above maximizes the possibility of resolving conflict with a win-win situation as opposed to the other two possible outcomes, win-lose or lose-lose. In a win-win scenario both (all) sides win, that is the needs of both sides are considered and both sides are satisfied their needs are met, both win. Win-win outcomes build trust and strengthen the organization. The other two scenarios have one or more loser. Losing is not an affirming experience. The winner might feel good but he should also watch his/her back. Losers have a tendency to look for and jump at an opportunity to get even. Losers may withdraw, and not be there for you or the organization in future trying times. Win-lose and lose-lose outcomes lead to mistrust and suspicion, lower morale and weaken the organization.

Conflict, well managed, is a good thing, to be embraced. It is the supervisor's friend.

Chapter 7

Decision-Making

The Great Equalizer

Do you know who said "My job is a decision-making job, and as a result, I make a lot of decisions?" Hint: he also said "I am the decider." It was President George W. Bush in a speech on the economy and job training on 10/4/2007. President Bush expounded upon the job of being a decision maker when on April 18, 2006 he defended keeping Donald Rumsfeld as Secretary of Defense, saying that he listened to all the voices (pro and con) and then made his decision (hold on to that thought for later on 'the decision- making process'). Decision- making is the great equalizer. Presidents do it. Supervisors do it. Line staff does it.

Life and work are full of decision-making occasions, many, minor, and some, major. How do you go about making decisions? Perhaps you use a Ouija Board, flip a coin, or pick one out of a hat (don't).

Decisions, Decisions, Decisions – Not

Some people take a vote, delegate (abdicate). Some experience what is called analysis paralysis, putting off making a decision while gathering more facts and information or, seeking out opinion after opinion. Some people find it hard to make decisions. It is a learned behavior. You can learn it and if you practice it, you can become good at it.

**HEADS -
FIRED**

**TAILS-
PROMOTED**

I never realized the negative impact lack of timely decision-making could have on an organization until I stepped into an acting director position a few years back. The first week on the job, as I met with each of my direct reports, each of them asked for a decision on one or more matters, some simple like a minor policy change, like implementing a new form, and some more serious with budget and service implications like adding new positions, raises, programmatic changes. One of the nicest compliments I have ever been paid was when after less than three weeks on that job, at a management staff meeting, one director with a smile on her face said "We've had more decisions made in the past three weeks than we've had in the past three years." Others at the meeting

PICK A CANDIDATE OUT OF THE HAT

SHOULD WE ELIMINATE THE THIRD SHIFT?

With permission from Josh Burke, Burke Networks

smiled and nodded in agreement. Those decisions, and many more to follow, were made using the very simple process about to be described. First, let's look at what decision-making is.

What Is It?

Decision-making is the act of selecting one from multiple options, opinions, or courses of action, using an intuitive or reasoned process, or frequently, a combination intuitive/reasoned approach.

Intuition relies on emotion and feeling, what your gut tells you. Intuition comes from your past life/work experiences and your own personal values/attitudes learned and reinforced over time, some at least, beginning in your childhood (which can cause you to be less objective, even blind when making decisions).

Reasoning relies on facts, data, and figures to make decisions. It is premised on objectively weighing all such information in order to make the best decision. Purely applied, it takes emotion out of the equation (like the expression goes, it's just business, not personal). Remember this, business decisions, like any decision, involve people and impact people, their feelings, and emotions. There are consequences to any decision. You would be wise to consider fact and feeling, yours and others, in making decisions.

For simple, routine decisions or when a quick decision must be made, intuition alone is fine. When decisions are more complicated I recommend using a structured approach involving both intuition and reason. You can find any number of decision-making methodologies online. There are many more similarities than differences among them. Such approaches better assure that important factors (facts and feelings) have not been overlooked and increase the likelihood of a successful outcome. In the paragraphs that follow I will describe my preferred approach.

Decision-Making Process: Another 12 Step Program

1. **Identify the issue, problem, opportunity.** Ask and answer such questions as:
   - What is the issue, problem, opportunity?
   - Why should it be of concern and or, addressed?
   - Who are the interested or affected parties?
   - Is there a deadline or timeframe for making the decision?

Commit responses to writing. I suggest you involve interested parties in answering these questions and share the draft statement of the issue, problem, or opportunity before proceeding to the other steps. It is best to be sure that all involved are on the proverbial same page at the beginning of the process. Get it wrong and time and resources may be wasted on the other steps.

2. **List the possible causes/reasons for the issue, problem opportunity.** Then prioritize the list. Put the prioritized list in writing and share and confirm with others involved in the process before moving to the next step (keeping everyone on the same page).

3. **Stop/Go Option.** Your intuition may be telling you something at this point. Based on the available information from Steps 1 & 2 above, is your gut telling you there is an obvious answer or solution? Perhaps the issue is not as significant or serious as you first thought. If you and those involved so far are comfortable making the decision now, trust your gut. If there is no consensus then move forward. If you're relatively inexperienced using a formal decision-making process, I recommend seeing the process through to the end anyway. As you become more experienced in using the process, you may feel comfortable cutting the process short here or further on in the process. If you do take a short cut and start questioning your decision after the fact, you can start over.

4. **Brainstorm.**
   - Compile a list of possible choices. Don't judge any at this time. Use as a rule of thumb that there is no dumb option.
   - This can be done individually with each participant submitting his/her list, or, in a group where a designated recorder lists them on a flip chart/white board.
   - Be sure to seek input from those you know will be affected

by the decision.

- Don't intend to identify all possible options. Set a timeframe for people to submit their lists to you. If compiling the list as a group exercise, set a time limit (probably no more than thirty minutes and stop sooner if there is a lull in responses).

5. **Gather information.**
   - For each possible choice on the list compiled in Step 4, ask what information is needed to evaluate it.
   - Identify where you can obtain the information.
   - Assign responsibility for obtaining the information.
   - Set a deadline for submitting information to you (or someone you designate) to compile this information for presentation to you, prior to moving on to Step 6.
   - Confirm with the decision-making group, mutual understanding of the information.

6. **Evaluate the facts/weigh the evidence.** Unlike Step 4, now is the time to judge.
   - For each of the options, review the information gathered, listing the pros and cons for each.
   - For each then ask the question "What might happen if this is chosen?"
   - Then ask the question "How likely is each choice to succeed?"
   - Ask if there is any further information that would be helpful based on responses to the three bullets above, and if you decide that such information is worth pursuing, gather it before proceeding.
   - If the matter is complex, it might be useful to use formal evaluation tools such as: a cost benefit analysis, force field analysis, starbursting, impact analysis, and/or futures wheel. For more information about these and other

evaluative tools, Google each or go to: https://www.mindtools.com/pages/article/newTED_00.htm

Note: I do not recommend these tools for the novice decision-maker. But as you gain more experience in decision-making and take on more complex decisions, you might want to learn more about them and selectively use them (but not your first time out of the gate).

7. **Choose!** This is a good time to interject your intuition.

- Review and/or discuss the information compiled in Steps 5 & 6.

- Which one or two alternatives stand out? Occasionally at this step a new alternative might surface or a combination of two or more alternatives may seem the best choice.

- As a confirming measure, ask what problems might result if chosen, what risks might result, who might resist the decision?

- Finally ask in your gut, does it feel right? If you are uncomfortable with the answer to the above three bullets, then go back to Step 4 and work the steps again from there.

8. **Go to Sleep.**

- If time allows, take time to reflect on the decision before announcing it to others. Once it becomes public it might be harder to change. After some rest and reflection (and time for yours and others' intuition to go to work), you may see it differently.

9. **Implement the decision.**

- Develop an implementation plan with assigned responsibilities, timeframes and resources and training.

- Announce the decision and plan to affected parties.

- Schedule Step 10.

10. **Review implementation.** Confirm whether or not the decision resolved the matter as defined in Step 1 and if so, at a satisfactory cost. If you find that it has not, go back and revisit starting with Step 1. Ask yourself if you learned anything that would improve future decision-making.

11. **Keep a record.** Keeping a record that you can refer to in the future increases your understanding of the whole process making it easier to manage future decisions. And it provides documentation of the process and the reasoning that went into the decision, should you or others question that decision down the line.

12. **Be guided by the Pareto Principle.** By now your head may be spinning and you may be talking to yourself, saying "I can't possibly go through all these steps for every decision I have to make." Go back and re-read the last paragraph under the heading "What Is It?" on the first page of this chapter. You don't have to and shouldn't use the process for every decision. Economist Wilfredo Pareto (1848 – 1923) developed the principle 80:20 (cited by Ivancic, 2014). Pareto found that 20% of the people in Italy held 80% of the wealth. It is widely accepted today that a small and shrinking majority of the population of the world holds the majority of the wealth. Pareto's principle remains true today. The principle has been applied to many disciplines since, including management. Many authors (Ivancic, 2014) writing about decision-making believe the majority of the decisions made at work are minor and not all that important, and can easily be made based on intuition and or, minimal reasoning. My own experience over the years confirms those claims. Most work decisions can and should be made without going through each of the first eleven steps above. There are other ways to approach decision-

making, for less important matters. You could be guided by policy and procedures that make the decision for you. You can look to past practices for similar matters. You can seek the advice of trusted staff or peers or consult an expert. If the decision can be made quickly in this manner and your own and others intuition feels that it is right, go with it. If your intuition and any reasoning you have done leaves you uncomfortable, then you should go through steps 1 through 11. As you become more comfortable using the full process, you will feel more comfortable in deciding when to use it and when not to use it.

Chapter 8

Hire Right (Smart), Fire Right (Timely)

Hire Right (Smart)

I believe many of a supervisor's personnel problems are a result of poor hiring on the supervisor's part, and/or on the part of his/her predecessor. Often, there is a rush to hire. You have good intentions. Perhaps you want to get the new person on board before the departing employee leaves to help with orientation and training; you want to ease the workload on staff that will have to cover the open slot; save on overtime; meet contract or licensing/accrediting standards; not do the work yourself; assure continuity of service. For any or all of these or other reasons, you might be inclined to settle for less than what you need or want to fill the slot. And if you have multiple openings, the likelihood of "settling" increases. You might get a superstar but you might get a dud. Bad hires will then need to be corrected later and can cause significant workplace discord, even harm. Tom Peters (2003, page 256) advises "Pursue the best... leave a job open... before you will fill a job with mediocrity... your legacy is one ... thing: the talent you beat the bushes to find and develop to get the job done." So my advice is: tough it out; hire smart. Here is how.

Assess the Vacant Position

If the vacancy is the result of a resignation, attempt yourself, or through a third party like the HR manager, to confirm exactly why the former or soon-to-be former employee is leaving. The stated reason may not be the real reason. If your organization doesn't have an exit interview policy, conduct one yourself. Take the opportunity to wish the departing employee well, thank him/her for her/his work; inquire about the new position or plans; obtain info on any work or projects that are pending, what their status is, and if there are any imminent deadlines; finally, ask if they wish to offer any suggestions for improving the workplace. Be aware that if the employee is leaving because of a conflicted relationship with you, he/she may be reluctant to offer negative feedback (a good reason to have HR or someone else conduct the interview). Such a meeting may not be what you think is the most important thing to spend your time on at the moment of an impending vacancy, but it will prove to be worth the effort. There may be an underlying problem in the workforce, which if not addressed can lead to job dissatisfaction on the part of the new hire, and you may end up with a revolving door. Start recruitment as soon as possible but be certain the job description accurately describes the position. Perhaps have the person leaving provide feedback on it; get feedback from other incumbents doing the same or similar job; have the HR manager review it. Consider if you want to take the opportunity of the vacancy to make any changes in the job description.

Advertise

Check your organization's policy or just work with the HR manager. You may be required to post the opening internally first for a specified time. If not, I prefer to post internally and advertise externally concurrently so as to identify a pool of candidates at the earliest opportunity. It is my preference to hire the best person for the job, giving preference to the internal candidate when an external and internal candidate appears equally suited. The internal candidate is a known entity, while the outside candidate is likely a stranger. Promoting from within, sends an important message to staff that there is room for growth for high performing employees. The process should then move from paper screening to interviews, to reference checks, to job offer.

Screen Applicants

Settle upon any criteria you want in candidates which are not already delineated in the job description. It is common for eager job applicants to submit their resumes for an open position for which they are not remotely qualified. A criteria checklist will make it easier to quickly eliminate those that do not meet the minimal criteria after an initial screening. Such a list will also help to eliminate those who are so overqualified you might be concerned about their long term commitment to the organization (taking this job while still pursuing other opportunities). You may prefer to screen all the applications yourself. That gives you better control but takes time that you might prefer to spend elsewhere. Perhaps the HR Manager can do the paper screening and forward applications that meet the criteria you set.

Conduct Interviews

Many management experts recommend multiple interviews and for good reason. Multiple interviews with different people and at different times of the day give you a better picture of the candidate. A second or third interviewer might get a different impression than you, and/or the candidate might interact differently with others. Further, he/she may behave differently at different times of the day, so schedule accordingly. Prepare before interviews. Settle upon a set of questions to be asked and use the same questions for all candidates (even for internal candidates). Be sure your questions are consistent with organization policy where such exists, and are legal. Review each applicant's paperwork before the interview and note areas to question (e.g., a gap in employment, multiple short stints, moving between completely unrelated jobs, reasons for leaving jobs). Ask the candidate what he/she knows of the organization and its mission, and how it lines up with his/her own values, interests and previous experience; you want to be confident that the candidate understands and will embrace the mission.

If you have the HR resources, I recommend letting HR conduct the first interview. After that, select candidates for a second interview but at a different time of day. That second interview could be with you and another person, perhaps a senior or trusted staff member in the department. Involving two people in the same interview gives you two opinions of the candidate. If you prefer, have a trusted department employee conduct the second interview and you could then do the third (final) interview. Have a specific set of questions for each set of interviews. Have each interviewer complete an interviewer form after each interview for your review. You may be interviewing a large pool of candidates over days, even weeks. Having such a form helps you keep track of who is who and what the interviewers' impressions were (remember the baseball saying "You can't tell the players without a scorecard"; the interviewer form is that scorecard). A sample Interviewer Form can be found at the end of this Chapter tiled The ABC Organization Employment Applicantion Summary.

If yours is a service-providing agency and the position is for front line staff, consider having an additional "interview" in which the candidate interacts with clients. You might be surprised at what is revealed, that did not come out on a carefully crafted resume or in a sterile interview environment. During the interview process, or at the end, if you prefer, sit down with all the interviewers to review and discuss the interviewer forms.

Narrow the Pool of Candidates and
Conduct Reference Checks

After considering the interviewers' feedback, ask if any of the candidates seem like a good match and rank them. Then ask yourself if the first choice meets your hiring criteria and if he/she seems like a good fit for the organization's culture and mission. Check and document the references. Also ask if the second and third choices are good matches. If your answer is yes, then you might want to have their references checked too to save some time (e.g., if the references for number one cause you to change your mind or if the first choice turns down the offer of employment). CAVEAT: Don't settle for number two or three. Ideally, you would be happy with any of your top choices and have a hard time ranking one over the other. But if that is not the case, don't settle for number two or three; continue the search process.

Extend the Job Offer and Confirm Acceptance

Most organizations have a policy that will determine who extends the offer and the process to be followed. If so you may have little to do other than indicate your choice to the HR representative. If there is no policy, this information will be helpful. Even if there is a policy, this information may be useful to you in influencing the content and delivery of the offer by HR.

Ideally, an offer will be received with enthusiasm and you can quickly start onboarding the person. Be prepared, however, if the offer isn't received favorably. The candidate may want to negotiate salary, benefits, time off, start dates, etc. Avoid disappointment and frustration by both employer and applicant by being clear from the point of initial application and throughout the interview process, on pertinent information such as current salary, job title, expected salary, availability to start and any already confirmed vacation plans, the date you need to have the position filled, hours and days of work, whether reference checking and drug/criminal background checks will be done, and the need to provide proof of legal eligibility to work. By the time you are ready to extend an offer you should have the answers to these questions. One variable to have clearly communicated early on in the process would be salary expectations. I recommend asking a salary range on the application. If it is higher than your budget allows but close enough, you can choose to continue with the process, making it clear to the candidate that it is more than you had in mind to offer, but that depending on their qualifications and how the interview goes, salary may be negotiable. It is also possible that the candidate will be attracted by the other benefits and accept the lower salary.

My preference is that a verbal job offer and request for acceptance should be extended first. There may be some negotiation of the terms and the need to allow time for the candidate to consider the offer. If the candidate wants time to consider the offer, set a deadline for an answer (24 hours is reasonable but 48 to 72 hours is not out of line). If the candidate accepts the offer, he/she should be congratulated, thanked for his/her interest in the organization, and informed that a formal written offer will be mailed within (fill in blank but next 24 to 48 hours is reasonable). Have the new hire sign both copies of it, keeping one for his/herself and returning the other (in a pre-addressed and stamped envelope).

The verbal and written offer should include salary, some statement of benefits (not in detail as usually the new employee will be selecting from various options e.g., health plans and retirement plans), start date, hours of work, vacation time, and where to report on the first day of work. If yours is an At-Will employment State, I recommend including a notice of that in the written confirmation letter with a further statement, that the letter notwithstanding, either party can terminate the relationship with or without cause.

If there is no organization policy specifying who makes the job offer, I generally recommend it be extended by HR and not the immediate supervisor. The exception would be for positions higher in the chain of command such as senior management, but even then I would have HR involved to be sure all organization policies and all applicable state and federal labor laws are followed. Allowing every supervisor to extend the offers independently will likely lead to confusion and inconsistencies in application of organizational policies, and increase the potential for labor disputes.

Have you heard this one? Reaching the end of a job interview, the Human Resources Officer asks a young engineer fresh out of the Massachusetts Institute of Technology, "And what starting salary are you looking for?" The engineer replies, "In the region of $125,000 a year, depending on the benefits package." The interviewer inquires, "Well, what would you say to a package of five weeks vacation, 14 paid holidays, full medical and dental, company matching retirement fund to 50% of salary, and a company car leased every two years, say, a red Corvette?" The engineer sits up straight and says, "Wow! Are you kidding?" The interviewer replies, "Yeah, but you started it." - See more at: http://www.laughfactory.com/jokes/office-jokes#sthash.XqskyGue.dpuf

Onboarding

Finish this sentence: If you've seen one onboarding program, you've _____. Did you answer "seen them all"? I suspect many, perhaps most choose that for an answer. I believe the correct answer, at this time at least, would be "seen one onboarding program". Why don't you test my hypothesis yourself? Google onboarding. I am confident you will find almost as many different onboarding programs as you find articles on the web.

Some will describe what you have always thought to be an employee orientation program, days to weeks long, 90 days at most (the proverbial probationary or introductory period). Others will run for six, nine, even twelve months, and some even up to two years. Some are informal, maybe initial paperwork and checklists of things to cover; maybe a scheduled sit down the first day and week or two; and then sort of "stop by anytime and let me know how you are doing or call me if you need me." Others are more formalized with a detailed schedule extending whatever length of time the program is. Some are a combination of a formal schedule and the informal understanding that either party can check now and then to see how the employee is doing and if he/she has questions or concerns.

One theory that has merit is that the longer the onboarding program, the greater the likelihood the employee will stay with the organization. The rationale is that it takes time for the employee to fully learn the job and the organization, its history, culture, organizational norms and way of doing things. The program needs to be long enough to cover such topics. I am not so sure that two years is necessary but I am pretty sure six months will not be long enough.

The onboarding process starts with the traditional orientation. Emphasis in orientation is the first day, and then the first one or two weeks, generally moving to scheduled meetings between the new hire and supervisor or HR designee for the first two or three months, to discuss how the employee is adjusting, areas of question, things the employee wants to learn and/or that the employer wants the employee to learn. Most often the first day is when outstanding paperwork is completed such as filling out tax forms, proof of legal eligibility to work, benefits selection, tour of the organization and worksite, and the basics, like time and attendance system/policy, work schedule, meal and breaks, where the bathroom. In the early days and weeks other topics are generally covered, like employee handbook, organizational history, products and services, mission etc. If onboarding ends here I believe the chances of the employee leaving within the first year of employment are higher than for employees that are offered a full onboarding program.

To help you understand the value of an extended onboarding program I offer this brief sociology lesson. One of the first terms I learned as an undergraduate sociology major was "socialization." At the same time I learned about norms, customs and values. The Wikipedia definition of "socialization" reads "lifelong process of inheriting and disseminating norms, customs, values and ideologies, providing an individual (new employee) with the skills and habits necessary for participating within their own society (participating in the formal and informal social structure of the organization)." Such socialization (aka onboarding) cannot be completed in a one- to three-month orientation process. New hires need an extended amount of time to learn by observing and listening to others in the workforce, checking on what he/she sees and hears to be certain it was correct, and to practice and become comfortable with the organizational way. Assigning the new hire to a buddy, perhaps one or more coaches, and/or a mentor (see references to coaching and mentors in chapter) in addition to scheduled trainings and supervision meetings will greatly assist in the new employee's onboarding/socialization into the organization.

All this may seem overwhelming to any supervisor, more so to a front-line supervisor. Don't panic. Check with HR or your own boss if you don't know what your organization has in place for orientation and onboarding. Don't assume someone else (e.g., HR) is handling it (as Felix Unger said in an Odd Couple skit "When you 'assume' you may make an ass of u and me"). Confirm what is in place and then add to it, especially as it pertains to the new employee learning of the organizational culture and norms that guide your particular unit.

Fire Right (Timely)

I am not recommending that you clean house. If you hire smart as recommended in the beginning of this chapter, and provide sufficient supervision, then occasions to fire those employees will be few and very far between. But unless yours is a new department, your workforce will initially, and for some time, be inherited from your predecessor. I refer you back to Chapter 3 "Meet and Greet...". That chapter speaks to getting to know your employees. As you get to know your employees you will see you have some that are outstanding; many who are solid and dependable; and some who are not performing at acceptable standards. It is likely, as you review personnel records, that you will find a discrepancy between what is in those folders (e.g., performance reviews, disciplinary action, etc), and your own assessment of their work performance. If that is the case, you can do something about it, or ignore it. Let's consider this further.

If you ignore it, what will happen? The job has to get done. If the sub-par performer is not doing it, someone else is (or it's getting neglected). You may take on some of the load, which can lead to stress for you and other staff. You may ask your outstanding employees to take on more. Initially, they may be enthusiastic, appreciating your recognition of their competence and commitment. But in short fashion they may start to be resentful, feeling put upon, get burned out and resentful to the point where their job performance suffers, or, they quit and you are going through that hiring process again. While this is going on, those sub-par employees are hearing a clear message, namely that their job performance is acceptable, good enough to just get a paycheck.

This situation is common in the workplace. Most people do not enjoy giving negative feedback and are reluctant to terminate someone, concerned about jeopardizing their livelihood, or afraid of being "the bad guy." Rather than be brutally honest in an annual review, many supervisors try to sugarcoat and make excuses for performance. This does not do any good for anyone or the organization. It reinforces in the mind of the sub-par employee that his/her poor performance is good, or good enough. It sends a message to the acceptable/solid employees that mediocrity is acceptable and that hard work will be rewarded with more work piled on. At the same time, outstanding employees may start to feel resentful for working as hard as they do, and it might lead them to do less, even leave. Drucker says "Executives [supervisors] who do not make the effort to get their people decisions right do more than risk poor job performance. They risk losing their organization's [employees'] respect" (2006, page 68).

I confess that I write all this as one who himself has been reluctant to tell sub-pars that their work is unacceptable, set clear measurable expectations of performance with timeframes, and hold them accountable. I found myself taking on others' workloads and asking my best employees to help pick up the slack. Sometimes I even explained to the outstanding employee, that I was depending on them because I could not depend on another, assured them I would work on holding the sub-par accountable, but failed to do so in a direct way. In fact I had one outstanding employee whom I was grooming as my possible successor on retirement, and lost him to resignation as he tired of picking up others slack while waiting for me to act. That loss convinced me to change my approach to supervising the sub-par employees in my last two years prior to retirement. The new strategies I used were effective. Here's how it works:

Develop a Work Improvement Plan (WIP)

If an employee's performance is sub-par (unacceptable) I seek to answer the question *why*. Tom Peters says "Weed out the rest" (2003, page 256), "Take reviews seriously" (2003, page 257), and "Set high standards" (2003, page 258). Some questions I ask myself include: does he/she have a job description and understand it; have they been trained as needed to do the task; do they have the proper tools/supplies to do the task? I then sit down with them (one on one, though you may at some point sit down with someone from HR as a witness) and ask them those questions. For any questions answered in the negative, I correct the situation, set in writing specific performance standards, and a timeframe for achievement and or follow-up (A Work Improvement Plan). Then I monitor the WIP and hold them accountable, which may solve the problem or bring me to firing. The desired outcome of a WIP is performance improvement. Absent follow-up and monitoring, most often the desired improvement does not occur (Effron, 2010, pages 101 & 102).

I don't know of anyone that enjoys firing an employee. If it is not something you enjoy doing and it is not something you do a whole lot, it is something you will always be uncomfortable doing, and all the more reason you should prepare for it. A friend of mine who is a principal in a private high school once told me he does not expel students but he does give some students the opportunity to be successful elsewhere. When firing employees, very frequently the firee gets emotional, makes excuses, claims you never gave him/her a chance, and were out to get him/her. Perhaps a different way of looking at it is that if I have been clear about the job and my expectations, provided necessary training and resources, and the employee (whether or not I hired him/her) still does not perform satisfactorily, then the employee fires him/herself, and I am just the messenger.

Follow-Up on the Work Improvement Plan and Do Not Put Off the Firing Decision

If the employee fails to satisfy the WIP, then termination is in order. It becomes a test of your integrity. Do you follow through on your word? You have been very clear to the employee what your expectations are; provided the training and resources; allowed time for improvement. It is clear the employee is not and will not be a good match, is not carrying his/her weight. It is an act of fairness to that employee, his/her co-workers, others impacted by his/her poor performance, and the organization. (Modifying the advice of my school principal friend, you may want to explore the possibility of another position in the organization that might be a better match for the employee's skills and interests but please, do not transfer your problem employee to another supervisor).

Follow HR Policy and Procedures on Termination

Save yourself a great deal of headaches (and perhaps wrongful discharge lawsuits) by being sure to follow HR policy on termination to the T. The actual firing should be handled in accordance with any written policy and procedures governing termination in your organization, and of course, in compliance with federal and state labor laws (possibly have a legal review before actually firing). I recommend a third party be present to observe and assist if needed. It should always be done in private. The employee should be informed that his/her performance continues to be unacceptable, which is not fair to others who have to pick up the slack, deal with his/her errors, attitude, etc. and so he/she is being terminated effective (put in date, usually immediately). Policy may allow you to pay the remainder of the day, the pay period and or, some other time (e.g., two weeks' severance). In giving any severance, be careful to treat people fairly lest you leave your organization open to a lawsuit

Firing Can Be Positive for All Concerned
Firing unsatisfactory employees serves multiple purposes. It can be a wake-up call for the fired employee. The awakening will be too late to save his/her job but it may motivate him/her to change so as to be successful in his/her next job. Even though you WILL NOT divulge to other employees that you fired someone, staff will put two and two together and be appreciative that they no longer are picking up the slack. Further, staff will know that you mean it when you set expectations. They know you are sincere when you tell them they are doing a good job when that compliment is not followed by dumping another's work on them. Such terminations give you the opportunity to hire another outstanding employee, raising the overall performance of your department and the morale too.

Hiring good employees and replacing poor performing employees with good employees (after giving them the opportunity to improve performance) will make your job as a supervisor much easier. Staff will support each other. Morale and motivation will be high. Less time will be taken on do-overs and supervising (disciplining) problem employees and smoothing over the ruffled feathers of the employees who have to pick up the slack of the poor performers. Everyone will have more time to create and maintain and improve upon the Dynamic Learning Organization covered in Chapter 11.

The ABC Organization Employment Application Summary

ABC ORGANIZATION - EMPLOYMENT APPLICANT ACTION SUMMARY

Name of Applicant	**Gender**	**Date of Application**

Position applied for: _____

Degrees: □ HS/GED   □ BA   □ MA   □ PhD

Application given to: _____ on _____

Name of staff	Date

Phone contacts with applicant on:	Outcome of contact:
1.	
2.	
3.	
4.	
5.	

□ Applicant scheduled for interview at _____ am/pm on _____

□ Applicant not appropriate for this position or any other at the ABC Org. Returned to Personnel Department on

_____. (Letter F)

□ Resume reviewed and applicant not appropriate for this position, but may be for another Program/Dept.

Returned to Personnel Dept on _____. (Letter B or D)

□ Applicant overqualified. Keep resume on file. Return to Personnel Dept on _____. (Letter E)

Applicant interviewed by: 1. _____ 2. _____

Rank applicant using the following scores:

1 = Above Average   2 = Average   3 = Below Average   4 = Beginner   5 = N/A

Scores		Scores	
	Professional appearance		Eye contact
	Experience		Insight
	Motivation		Written skills
	Knowledge of job		Potential for promotion
	Estimated ability to complete written work		Estimated ability to handle caseload

□ Interview offered position; will begin work on _____ at a salary rate of _____. (Letter A)

□ Applicant not being offered position. (Letter D)

□ Applicant declined position because _____ (Letter C)

This form completed by _____ Date: _____

(Continued on other side)

A   Letter confirming that <u>interviewee</u> has been hired:

We enjoyed meeting you and are delighted that you have accepted a position as a _____ at ABC

Organization. This letter confirms that we have offered this position to you and that you will begin work at ABC on _____/_____/_____ at _____.

We look forward to having you join our staff. In the meanwhile, if you have any questions, please feel free to call me.

B   <u>Interviewee</u> that we are not hiring, but want to keep on file for future:
Thank you for interviewing for a position at ABC Organization. We enjoyed meeting with you and appreciate your interest in us. Unfortunately, we had a number of strong candidates apply and we are not able to offer you a position at this time. We will keep your resume in our open file for the next six months and will contact you then we have an opening.

C   <u>Interviewee</u> who was offered position, but declined:
Thank you for taking the time to interview with us and for sharing so much information about yourself. I enjoyed learning about you in this way. I am sorry that we are not able to meet your expectations for this position. We would have been pleased to have you on our staff and hope that you will consider ABC Organization for any future openings that may be more in keeping with your requirements.

D   <u>Applicant</u> whose resume we will keep on file, but are not interested in for this position:
Thank you for submitting your resume for employment at ABC Organization. Unfortunately, the position we currently have open is not suitable for the background you present. We will keep your resume in our active file for the next six months and will contact you should there be a suitable opening. We wish you luck with your job search.

E   <u>Applicant</u> who is too qualified for position and whose resume we will keep active:
Thank you for submitting your resume for employment to ABC Organization. Unfortunately, we have no openings at this time that are suitable for someone with your impressive qualifications. We will keep your resume and application in our active file for the next six months and will contact you should there be a suitable opening.

F   <u>Applicant</u> that we neither want to interview nor keep their resume inn open file:
Thank you for submitting your resume to ABC Organization. Unfortunately, we had a number of strong candidates apply for this position and we are not able to offer you an opportunity to interview. We appreciate your in interest in ABC and wish you good luck with your job search.

G   <u>Applicant</u> who has submitted an unsolicited resume or application that is a good candidate but we have no openings:
Thank you for submitting your resume to ABC Organization. Unfortunately there are no openings for this position for which you applied at this time. We will keep your application in our open file for six months and will contact you should a suitable opening occur.

H   Unsolicited resume/application that we do not want to consider for employment:
Thank you for submitting your resume to ABC Organization. Unfortunately we have no openings that are suitable for you at this time. We appreciate your interest in the agency and wish you good luck with your job search.

Have You Heard This One?
(about the 100 Bricks Job Hiring Process)

Here is the problem:
HOW DO YOU RECRUIT PEOPLE INTO A BUSINESS?
See the answer below:
Put about 100 bricks in some particular order in a closed room with an open window.

Then send 2 or 3 candidates in the room and close the door.

Leave them alone and come back after 6 hours and then analyze the situation.

If they are counting the bricks, put them in the accounts department.

If they are recounting them, put them in auditing.

If they have messed up the whole place with the bricks, put them in engineering.

If they are arranging the bricks in some strange order, put them in planning.

If they are throwing the bricks at each other, put them in operations.

If they are sleeping, put them in security.

If they have broken the bricks into pieces, put them in information technology.

If they are sitting idle, put them in human resources.

If they say they have tried different combinations, yet not a brick has been moved, put them in sales.

If they have already left for the day, put them in marketing.

If they are staring out of the window, put them on strategic planning.

And then last but not least, if they are talking to each other and not a single brick has been moved,

Congratulate them and put them in top management.

From Really Funny Clean Jokes and Humor. http://www.tensionnot.com/jokes/office_jokes/100_bricks_job_hiring_process

Chapter 9

Supervising – Do It!

Philosophy of Supervision

There are many styles of management. Some styles are more suited to different situations. A participatory style, emphasizing collaboration and participatory decision-making is widely viewed as a good approach to management and ordinarily is my preferred approach. But it's not the approach I used on the morning of September 11, 2001. It is not the approach I use in a crisis. On 9/11/2001, I was sitting at my desk, planning my day's activities as the president of Catholic Charities in Paterson NJ (a thirty minute ride from the World Trade Center) when the phone rang. One of my staff, Sr. Maria, informed me that a plane had just crashed into the World Trade Center.

My first step was to make some calls to confirm the information, and assess the need for help. My second step was to call a leadership team meeting post haste but not for the purpose of developing a collaborative plan of response. The meeting was called for two purposes. The first was to inform them of the situation as I understood it. The second purpose was to delegate responsibilities giving very specific directions aimed at letting our donors and supporters and the general public know what they could do to help and to reach out to contacts at and near ground zero to offer help and continuously assess their needs. Quickly, I moved back into the participatory/collaborative mode myself and through designated staff, to further plan our immediate and long term response.

I cite the above to illustrate my personal belief that the better supervisors will have a preferred management style but should be able to adjust that style to the needs and situations as they present themselves. I invite you to Google the subject of supervisory style to learn about the many approaches. Add such readings to your personal reading list. This could be the start of a plan to strengthen your style or change it). As you learn about your own management style and as you get to know your workforce, you will begin to adjust your approach to dealing with different situations and personalities (see Chapter 14). Look for educational opportunities on the subject. The range of styles go from the boss who says jump and you jump or ask how high, to the boss who asks your take and advice on the matter at hand, to some combination of the two extremes.

I already told you in the second paragraph above that my preferred style is a participatory/collaborative one. I want to describe how I supervise from this framework. I am not saying that you should supervise in exactly the same way as I do. You should develop an approach that you are comfortable with, that best serves your supervisees, helping them grow, and, that will work for you in your organization's culture. Perhaps some of what I do might appeal to and work for you. You may want to try some or others that you read about as a sort of trial and error approach.

The Act of Supervising A La Joe Duffy – Another 12 Step Program

1. **I meet with my direct reports for a regularly scheduled monthly meeting at a day and time convenient for both parties.** I am careful to avoid scheduling such meetings at the time of day I am least productive (which for me is in the mid afternoon when I might be at risk of dozing off or zoning out). It is understood that I am available PRN in between meetings and I tell staff not to hold a pressing issue for the regular meeting, rather pop in or call. I schedule these meetings as a means to assure minimal contact with staff, for mutual sharing and updating, and monitoring progress and goals and assignments. I use a standing agenda including progress on goals, projects,

budget status, mission and main thing discussion and review, what is on your mind and plate, how can I help you, how can you help me and/or the organization. Monthly meetings have worked for me. I schedule more frequent meetings for new hires until both of us are comfortable meeting less often. Some supervisors like to have more frequent individual meetings. Others prefer less structure as in I call or you call as needed/desired.

2. **I also meet with direct reports as a group once a month and similarly schedule as in Step 1.** The standing meeting is on everyone's calendar. I send out a proposed agenda a few days in advance, inviting staff to add to it. The final agenda is sent out at least a day in advance. We have agreed upon ground rules for these (and all) meetings. Generally they include, start on time; end on time (or early); come prepared as in if there was an assignment from the prior meeting or on the agenda, have a progress report and/or do the reading; one person talks at a time; no yelling; no vulgarity; disagreement is allowed, even encouraged, but no personal attacks. Meetings are generally used to update each other on their respective areas of responsibility, policy review and discussion, education, budget review, and problem-solving. I email brief minutes of these meetings within 24 hours of each meeting. It is good to have a record as evidence and for ease of follow-up. Meeting as a group more or less often is at your discretion. As I checked out of a hotel once, I made a point of telling the front desk manager how pleased I was with the customer service of a particular housekeeping staff member. That manager asked my permission to share my compliment with that person in front of her staff at their morning staff briefing. Depending on the nature of your work, a daily group meeting or briefing may be helpful.

3. **I maintain an open-door (modified) policy.** I keep my office door open as an invitation for folks to walk in. I tell staff they can always stop by or call PRN if they have a need to, rather than hold a pressing matter or burning question for the next scheduled meeting (balance this against time distractions covered in the chapter on time management). Staff also know that if my door is closed, I prefer not to be interrupted unless it is an emergency. And if staff does interrupt and I do not see the matter as an emergency, I let the person know same, lest I reinforce such is acceptable.

4. **Communicate frequently and with variety.** Use a variety of communication tools (see chapters on communication). If something is important say it, say it again, and say it again but differently using different tools. Realize how different people respond to different forms of communication and when possible communicate to them in their preferred style. Attempt to share as much information as possible balancing what people want and need to know against privacy, confidentiality and legal concerns.

5. **Praise in public.** There is much truth to the saying "You get the behavior you reward." People respond to praise. Positive reinforcement makes the recipient feel good about him/herself and sends the person the message that he/she is doing something well or right. Specific praise builds confidence (Blanchard, 2015, page 32). I believe when praise is given publicly, it is even a stronger reinforcement. It has the added benefit of encouraging others hearing the praise to want to emulate such behavior and possibly be the recipient of such praise in the future. Praise is most effective when it is specific. Rather than speak in generalities like saying Mary's speech was great,

the praise should include specifics about why you thought the speech was great. As often as I can, I attempt to give praise as close as possible to the event. The immediacy of the reinforcement increases its effectiveness. When you can, consider dual or multiple modalities. On occasion I have sent a person a personal note specifying the praise I am offering, announced the same at a staff meeting and concurrently sent a mass email. For example after a State inspection of a licensed drug treatment program I ran, I sent a personal and tailored thank you to the key persons that made the visit a success, sent a mass email to the entire agency announcing the results, singling out particular people, and publicly acknowledged those people at the exit interview with the State team. I also kept a copy of any positive feedback in that employee's personnel file for use at annual review time. So praise often. If you "do it twice as often as you think you should... you'll have a good chance of meeting your employees' needs" (Cottrell, 2003, page 26).

6. **Criticize in private.** Some people criticize in public, possibly as a teaching moment to discourage others from such failure, possibly to embarrass the person to change a behavior, and/or maybe (and hopefully not) because you like to exercise power that way. Criticizing in public may cause immediate compliance, but it also may demoralize that employee and others, and cause a toxic non-productive work environment. Providing negative feedback is a necessary part of the job. It can be helpful to the employee pointing out what was wrong, and/or how and why something can be done better. Blanchard (2015, page 47) calls this "One Minute Re-Direct" emphasizing the importance of ending such sessions by emphasizing your trust in them and support for their success. Constructive

feedback helps the employee grow and helps to create and maintain a positive work environment. I also keep a copy of constructive criticism in the employee's personnel file for use at review time and for ongoing monitoring of job performance.

7. **Performance Reviews.** In every organization I have worked, employees received an annual performance review. I offer a caveat. I believe an annual review is a useful and necessary tool. It is that time of year to formally review the entire year and to set goals for maintaining and improving performance and growing in the next year. But an employee should always know how he or she is doing. The annual review should be a confirmation of what the supervisor and employee already know, not a surprise. Performance should be part of the scheduled individual and group meetings, part of informal PRN meetings that occur throughout the year, and be reflected in the occasions for positive and negative feedback documented all year long. I offer a second caveat. Do not hope bad performance will improve if ignored or talked around. Deal with it timely, directly, and specifically (see Chapter 8 Hire Right, Fire Right). Doing so is the fair and right thing to do for that employee, his/her co-workers, clients and the organization.

8. **Be fair not necessarily equal.** When I have spoken at employee orientations I would tell the new hires that everyone will be treated fairly in accordance with policy and law and without favoritism. Employees have different needs at different times and they have different capabilities. If for example I were to treat everyone equally then in terms of monthly individual meetings, everyone would be allotted the same time. In fairness though

some employees might only need a fraction of an hour a month and others the full hour. I give them the time they need. Some employees need more time to complete an assignment than another. So long as deadlines can be met, I allow for such differences (of course looking for ways to improve the productivity of the slower person).

9. **Reward.** One form of reward was already addressed above "praise in public." Praise is a very effective reward tool. There are others. I have been offered tickets to plays and sporting events. I have given them to staff as a reward. While staff may appreciate the recognition of receiving those hockey tickets, if they hate hockey, the reward is less effective. So attempt to confirm what reward is effective for which employee, be it a book, a movie, dinner, sporting event, day off, tee shirt, special parking place, gift card, etc.

10. **Manage By Walking Around (MBWA).** I have been a proponent of MBWA throughout my career. I don't think a day has gone by that I did not purposely get up from my desk and walk around (and often drive around to our different locations). For much of my career I had responsibility for one or more 24 hour operations. In such situations I would schedule time for MBWA on other shifts. MBWA is the perfect tool for communicating (talking and listening), a way to help keep your finger on the pulse of the organization, testing mission awareness and telling others how the organization is doing.

11. **Ask "How am I doing?"** Three-term New York City Mayor Ed Koch was famous for his trademark question "How am I doing?" While he frequently asked his constituents the question, some critics say he often did not listen. You need to know how you are doing so you can take positive steps

to improve. So ask that question of yourself and others often. Very importantly, listen to and act on the answers. See Chapter 13 ahead for suggestions on how to do this.

12. **Be a person of integrity.** Being a person of integrity means doing the right thing at all times, even when no one is watching (how do you know when no one is watching or listening). If you are not a person of integrity, people will lose trust in you. If people do not trust you, they will not follow you (for long). If people trust you they will give you their proverbial right hand, follow you to hell and back, ask how they can help, improve the work environment.

Chapter 10

Time Management

A Time Manager's Prayer

The Serenity Prayer is suited for many uses, among them, time management. So, let us pray: Lord, grant me the serenity to accept the things I cannot change; the courage to change the things I can; and the wisdom to know the difference. This prayer, written by American theologian Reinhold Niebuhr in the early 20th century and later adopted by Alcoholics Anonymous and other 12 step group meetings, is a good prayer for all of us in our work and personal lives. I think it is particularly pertinent to the subject of this chapter. If you don't accept the things you cannot change, rather than the experience of serenity, you will likely find yourself stressed, anxious, and eventually burnt-out. Changing the things you can is equally important, and lacking the courage to do so will result in the same consequences as failing to accept what you cannot change. Some changes will be easy to make in the way you manage your time, but others, such as saying "no" to current and future demands on your time, may take courage. Cultivating the wisdom to know the difference will help you to better manage your precious time and avoid wasting it. It is easy to mistakenly think you can change something that you really have little control over, and if stubbornness is a particularly strong character trait, you may be more prone to this misjudgment. Failure to know the difference not only wastes time, it can undermine your self-confidence, weaken your credibility with your employees, and perhaps most importantly, delay actions in trying to change the things you can change (Chapter 7 Decision-Making will help you in finding the wisdom to know the difference).

When a 24 Hour Day is not Enough

Have you ever heard it said (or said it): Where did the day (hours/time) go; Time sure flies; There's just not enough hours in the day; The hour got by me; When things slow down or when I have a few minutes I am going to...? Such sayings are examples of becoming slaves to time, of time management out of whack. And all too often, improvements in technology, billed as a useful tool in saving or managing time, do just the opposite. Cell phones and email have made it possible to be available 24/7. Some bosses expect you to be available that way, thereby robbing you of precious personal/family time. Checking and responding to emails throughout the day take up a lot more time than was spent dealing with the once a day US mail delivery and the once or twice a day inter-office mail delivery. I suspect that as technology advances further with added and/or improved tools for communicating, things will get out of hand. Have you ever said or heard someone say "That was a waste of time"? Keep this question in mind as you read ahead about taking action after your time management inventory and analysis. Asking this question about each of the activities in your time management inventory and following up by asking why for those activities, might inform your corrective action and make you a better time manager. Failure to manage your time effectively can lead to stress, anxiety, mistakes, job dissatisfaction and unhappiness. Fear not! Time management isn't rocket science. It's a learned (easily learned) behavior. Pray that serenity prayer, learn, and then practice good time management techniques. Let us begin.

Step Time Management Recovery Program

1. **The first step is to admit you don't control the use of your time as well as you need or want, and conduct an inventory of how you spend your time.** Your first reaction

might be that this action step places even more demands on your time; throw your hands up; and continue the status quo. Investing this time up front will save you more time in the end. As you document how you spend your time, you will see what activities you do day in and day out and be able to analyze those activities. That analysis will help you to identify how your time is organized (or not); question their importance; consider how they are placed in your calendar vis-a-vis your energy level; identify interruptions and other time wasters and start a thought process about how you might better schedule your day, e.g., matching more important activities to that time of day when you have the most energy, and/or have the least interruptions; even how you can eliminate or lessen interruptions. Drucker said "Time is the scarcest resource, and unless it is managed, nothing else can be managed" (2001, Page 51).

So how do you conduct a Time Management Inventory? Keep a paper or computer log or diary of your day, including the start and stop time for each activity you do, a brief description of that activity, and its importance. Document the source of any interruption and the relative importance of that interruption. Most time management consultants recommend you collect this information for two weeks to establish a good baseline of how you manage your time. I recommend the same, at least for first timers. I believe less time would be sufficient, perhaps a week, for repeat offenders with the caveat that you are comfortable that the week you choose is a fairly typical work week.

Take advantage of one of the many online forms available to help you conduct your inventory. It makes it easier for you to document your time; categorize activities; identify interruptions and other time wasters and begin to visualize how you spend your day. I've used the form below for years when teaching time management skills to groups or working individually with one of my direct reports. After all these years, I do not recall if I developed it from scratch or adapted from other sources. Wanting to find out if someone else developed it, I Googled time management forms but couldn't find it, but I did find other similar forms, you can choose. I like the form below. It provides a format to keep a time management log/diary, rate the importance of each item to your work, match interruptions to activities and time of day, and identify the source and nature of interruptions. All of this information will be helpful in developing your time management action plan.

DAILY TIME LOG

DATE _____

TIME	ACTIVITY	*IMPORTANCE		INTERRUPTIONS		
				Tele	Other	Nature
6:00		+ − ? 1 2 3 4 5				
6:30		+ − ? 1 2 3 4 5				
7:00		+ − ? 1 2 3 4 5				
7:30		+ − ? 1 2 3 4 5				
8:00		+ − ? 1 2 3 4 5				
8:30		+ − ? 1 2 3 4 5				
9:00		+ − ? 1 2 3 4 5				
9:30		+ − ? 1 2 3 4 5				
10:00		+ − ? 1 2 3 4 5				
10:30		+ − ? 1 2 3 4 5				
11:00		+ − ? 1 2 3 4 5				
11:30		+ − ? 1 2 3 4 5				
12:00		+ − ? 1 2 3 4 5				
12:30		+ − ? 1 2 3 4 5				

* Importance can rate from 1 to 5 with a 1 being very important and 5 unimportant.

Or circle + for productive, - for lost or wasted or ? for undecided or questionable.

DAILY TIME LOG

DATE _____

TIME	ACTIVITY	*IMPORTANCE	INTERRUPTIONS		
			Tele	Other	Nature
1:00		+ – ? 1 2 3 4 5			
1:30		+ – ? 1 2 3 4 5			
2:00		+ – ? 1 2 3 4 5			
2:30		+ – ? 1 2 3 4 5			
3:00		+ – ? 1 2 3 4 5			
3:30		+ – ? 1 2 3 4 5			
4:00		+ – ? 1 2 3 4 5			
4:30		+ – ? 1 2 3 4 5			
5:00		+ – ? 1 2 3 4 5			
5:30		+ – ? 1 2 3 4 5			
6:00		+ – ? 1 2 3 4 5			
6:30		+ – ? 1 2 3 4 5			
7:00		+ – ? 1 2 3 4 5			
7:30		+ – ? 1 2 3 4 5			
8:00		+ – ? 1 2 3 4 5			
8:30		+ – ? 1 2 3 4 5			

* Importance can rate from 1 to 5 with a 1 being very important and 5 unimportant.
Or circle + for productive, - for lost or wasted or ? for undecided or questionable.

2. **Analyze your time management log in the spirit of the second phrase of the Serenity Prayer, "the courage to change the things I can" looking to identify things to eliminate, and/or things you can do differently (more effectively and or more efficiently –better/faster).** For each listing in your log, ask that question "Was that a waste of time?" Your answer could lead to a decision to discontinue that activity or otherwise change it, e.g., eliminate a report or meeting. It might be possible to delegate it to someone else, freeing you of that activity and providing another, a growth opportunity (caution, if you delegate be sure the person has the time to take it on, has the resources to do it, receives proper training, and, very importantly, do not micro-manage the person – let it go).You will likely find in your inventory that you are doing some things because they have always been done that way, and you are uncertain why, or what their value is. In your analysis you want to get that answer and then act accordingly.

As you answer that question "Was this a waste of time?" you will find activities that are necessary but did waste time and should be done differently. You will find some activities though not a waste of time still could be done differently resulting in better use of your time. Using the same example as in the above paragraph, you could shorten a report or meeting, or change the frequency of either, perhaps from monthly to quarterly. When answering the question "Was this a waste of time?" use the organization's mission and vision statement and any "main thing" statements (more on "main thing" statements in Chapter 12 on work environment) as a yardstick to measure its usefulness.

In the position I retired from in 2016, at one time, I chaired six Boards. Some of those boards met monthly, some every other month, and one met ten times a year. By the time I retired, the total number of Boards was reduced from six to three. Two of the three Boards switched to quarterly meetings and the third meets every other month with a break in July and August. This was made possible by amending the bylaws clause about meeting frequency, adding a clause allowing for mail/email votes in-between meetings, settling upon interim reports and data to be shared with board members between meetings, and delegating some responsibilities to committees. There were significant time savings not only for me in not having to attend (travel to and from) so many meetings and prepare for them, but as well, there were time savings for staff that had to prepare for and attend those meetings. And of course, no Board member complained about having freed up more of their time.

Another suggestion that might increase the effectiveness of your analysis of your time management log would be to have a trusted co-worker (not necessarily in your own department) review your inventory and analysis and provide you feedback. If you have a secretary, he/she probably knows you better than most of your other staff and so would be a good choice. If there is no one at work you are comfortable asking, you might want to ask someone outside of work, perhaps a friend/family member. This person might have feedback that would cause you to further consider your analysis, and/or he/she might have other thoughts worthy of your consideration that might help you construct an even stronger plan of action. You might want to seek feedback in this way again, in constructing or reviewing your plan of action in the next step of improving your time management.

Each of the steps that follow below offer ways to better manage your time by eliminating some activities, and/or doing them in a different (more efficient way).

3. **Plan your day in advance.** Use a desk calendar planner, a pocket version or, if you are computer savvy, use a computer calendar. Microsoft Office is but one of many that allows you to schedule, receive meeting reminders, keep notes, and more. Start the day with some uninterrupted time to review your calendar, update it, and maintain a to-do list. Prioritize activities by importance and/or must do (that is, of a long list of things to do, put the priorities first to better insure they get done). Look at the end of the list, and ask yourself about those towards the end - should they even be on the list? Check off items as they are done. Even though I use an electronic calendar, I always keep a little piece of paper in my shirt pocket and write myself notes on it. Family and friends know not to buy me a dress shirt sans pocket. I exchanged the last such shirt I received. My wife is not so happy with this practice as I also keep a pen (which occasionally leaks, especially when I forget to retract the point). I have the ability to make my own hours so arrive to work early before the day shift starts. That leaves me plenty of quiet uninterrupted time to plan my day, check files and messages. You can end your day by reviewing what was accomplished and not, update calendars and to do lists. The above references the daily calendar but each day as you plan, be looking ahead and mark your calendar days, weeks, months ahead etc. I concentrate on such forward planning at the beginning of the work week, but update as needed.

4. **Avoid cluttered desk syndrome.** A cluttered desk is one where things get forgotten (often things with deadlines attached to them), forgotten about altogether (out of sight, out of mind), or get misplaced, taking extra time to look for them when needed. Keep your desk clear of clutter. Process paper only once. It is not always easy or

even possible to process paper only once, but it is possible more often than not. I use four things to help control my desk clutter. I keep an "in and out box" on my desk. When things arrive (like interoffice mail, hand delivered memos, US mail), they go into my inbox (if not an actual box/ tray, a pile on the desk), and an out box with items for my secretary to file or otherwise dispose of (when not obvious I put a post-it note on the item with the instruction), and outgoing mail for posting at one or more intervals during the day. I keep a tickler file in my office. In a file cabinet I have a set of file folders numbered 1 through 31, a set of 12 folders labeled January through December, and a folder labeled next year. Rather than have papers pile up on my desk, I will place them strategically in one of these folders to be handled at the appropriate time. If it is July and the next month starts, I pull the August folder contents and distribute them into the 1 through 31 labeled folders and so on as each month and each year changes. I also maintain a file divider on my desk with folders labeled for what I consider active matters so that I do not have to keep running to a file cabinet somewhere to retrieve such active paperwork every time I need to work on it. And last but very important, I have a large trash basket (often called the circular file). I really try to throw out what can be chucked (my basket is sometimes emptied twice a day).

There are a very few exceptions to the clutter rule. Pictured below is the desk of one of two people I have worked with over the past 45 years whose desk is cluttered, yet who can find anything on it in seconds. For them this is organized. So perhaps you may be that exception. If so, beware of well-meaning folks that try to organize for you or strong winds that blow papers away and topple your piles.

This is the desk of the CFO where I worked prior to retirement.
He could locate anything on it in seconds. He is the exception
to the rule. You probably aren't, so don't try this.

Unfortunately, there is no test I know of to identify who
is the exception to the rule. If you think you are such an
exception, you may want to give it a try, but there is a
good chance you will be wasting yours and others' time.

5. **Organize your calendar and to do list action times
around your biorhythms.** Understand your body and
your mind. Are you a morning person? If so, then plan
to work on the most important items in the morning. If
you leave the difficult things till later in the day, they will
likely weigh on your mind and be a distraction; may cause
you to take longer to complete other tasks, even make
mistakes leading to having to do things over and wasting
even more time. I am a morning person. In fact, there are
times in the afternoon that I could easily nod off and so I
avoid scheduling group meetings and try to avoid being
scheduled into such meetings later in the day, for fear of
doing just that, nodding off (I've done it). If I cannot avoid
such, I might ask a trusted person to sit by me and give

me a kick. When such times occur. I might take a proactive measure such as going for a power walk (works well with MBWA), hit the bathroom and splash water on my face, stand up and stretch and take a few deep breaths, have a caffeinated beverage, and/or open a window or turn the A.C. up. Most of us slow down and feel a bit fatigued after lunch (avoid turkey). Be aware of this if you are one of those folks, in planning your day (and if you cannot control for it, eat light and avoid alcohol). Changing your lunch hour can provide you added time each day. If you go earlier or later than most of your co-workers, you will spend less time on lines waiting to be served or pay and you will have less interruptions while working because more people who would be the likely interrupters are eating while you are working.

6. **Group (batch work when you can).** Try to make and return calls in one chunk of time, check and respond to emails at one chunk of time, open mail at one chunk of time, and write or dictate correspondence at one chunk of time. In this way, there is let time spent, organizing and setting up such work, and putting things away after, and transitioning from activity to activity. Mentally you are more prepared working with such batches.

7. **Control your email and phone.** Don't let them control you. You don't check your US mail throughout the day. You know when your US mail is expected each day and deal accordingly. But email comes at you all day long. That does not mean you have to open every email as it comes in. You don't need to respond immediately. In fact, if it is your habit to respond as the message arrives you are reinforcing with the sender that they can email at any time and expect a quick response. If they don't get a

quick response, they might resend the message or call you, taking up more of your precious time and theirs. So don't spoil them. Consider turning off the alarm notifying you "you got mail" on your phone and desk top. Discipline yourself to check and respond to emails at a few specified times each day. Let your people know that (train them). When they do the same, respect their practice. Everyone will have time to spend doing something else. When out of the office for an extended period of time, e.g., for a whole or partial day meeting, have an automated response inform the sender of that and when you will be back, if possible offering an alternative if they need a response sooner, such as "if you cannot wait for my return, email (fill in blank), call (fill in blank)", or if you really want to be bothered, give them your cell (which no doubt they will keep forever and use –taking up more of your time and distracting you from important things, like golf or family dinner). When you are out of office, especially for multiple days, ask your secretary to check on your email and when possible, handle it, but let you know what she/he does with it. When returning from vacation try to come in early the first day back, to catch up and if possible leave your calendar free or only lightly filled.

If you have the phone ringing at your desk throughout the day, there will be one interruption after another. Use the capabilities that your phone system offers. Perhaps have your phone forward to a secretary or a co-worker who on a scheduled or occasional basis, forward his/her calls to you (help each other manage time). Have the phone automatically go to voice mail and at set times of the day listen and respond, better yet, if you have secretarial support have him/her check your messages and handle what she can, reporting actions to you. When returning from vacation try to come in early the first day back, to catch up and if possible leave your calendar free or only lightly filled.

8. **Plan for vacation or multiple day conferences.** Put in extra time for a few days before you will be out of office to get things done to help avoid being overwhelmed when you return. Arrange for trusted employees to handle certain matters and respond on your behalf to messages or problems as they occur, including checking and managing your phone and email messages. While it is wise to avoid doing work on vacation it might help you mentally be more involved in vacation and benefit from it, if you take a limited amount of time each day to check your email, your voice mail, or call the office (but limit that, perhaps no more than twice a day, and certainly for no more than an hour, tops). In this way, you still enjoy vacation but do not feel so overwhelmed your first day back.

9. **Avoid and control distractions.** Let people know that certain times are your quiet time to think, plan and get things done (including turning off electronic devices – go off the grid). It is widely known at work, among family and friends that I am at my desk very early each morning. It is also widely known that I like to have this time uninterrupted so I can better concentrate. I expect folks to respect my wish and let them know I will respect their quiet time (I refer to this as sacred time and encourage others to publicize their sacred time). Clarify (modify) your open-door policy if you have one. I frequently say my door is always open, as a way to encourage communication. People do not need an appointment to see me. But over time I learned to clarify my open-door policy, lest people think it is absolute and they have the right to barge in unannounced anytime. I suggest, when they can,

staff should call first or schedule a time to see me so as not to waste their time coming to my office only to find me not there or otherwise occupied. Even though a phone or face to face conversation is not confidential I will often close my office door. A closed door sends a message not to disturb. Sometimes, I may even put a sign on my closed office door, indicating I am working on something, and asking them to come back later or make an appointment but saying if it cannot wait, to knock and interrupt. If someone chooses to interrupt and in your opinion the matter could have waited, it would be important to give the person that feedback so that they do not continue such a pattern of needlessly interrupting. While you want to be a gracious host, you don't want to encourage interrupting behaviors. When someone walks in and you have or are about to do something, stand and remain standing. If you stand, they will stand, not settle in and likely finish what they have to say and be on their way. When someone comes into your office or stops you elsewhere at work and opens with "Have you got a minute?" do not hesitate to be honest. I will on occasion say no as I have an appointment to leave for now, or am expecting an appointment momentarily. Or I might say "If it is literally a minute I can, but if not I can't" for the same reason, perhaps telling them when I will be available or offering to schedule a time to meet.

If in analyzing your time management log you identify particular people that are repeatedly interrupting, deal with it. Schedule time to sit privately with the person(s). Tell them about your effort to manage your time better and share the data about the number of interruptions and nature. Assure the person(s) you want to be available to them but need to better control interruptions so you can be more effective. Ask if they have any suggestions about how to limit interruptions but be prepared to add any or all of the following and any other reasons you can think of: You might just remind the person(s) of specific times of the day you can be reached as needed; suggest they call and leave a message or send an email which you can respond to later (explain how you handle email and phone messages); ask if questions can be held for the next regular scheduled meeting; ask if questions could be grouped and asked at one time of the day, rather than multiple times throughout the day.

11. **Strategically arrange your office furniture.** If your chair faces the door and your door is open or has a window frame, people will see you are in and knowing you have that open-door policy, will be more likely to pop in anytime. Having a bird's eye view from your chair can be a source of interruption even when people do not come in. You are seeing the world pass by so to speak and that can be distracting.

12. **And then there are meetings.** While I do say "That was a good meeting" and have heard others say "That was a good meeting" I also have said and heard said "I hate meetings" or "That meeting was a waste of time" even more often. Needless or bad meetings waste not only your time, but the time of most if not all in attendance. What a waste!!!! Here are my tips on meetings:

- Ask the question "Was that a waste of time?" when analyzing meetings recorded in your time management log. If you answer yes, do something about it (some of the tips that follow will be of help). Don't just ask that question when analyzing your time management log; ask it routinely at the end of meetings. There are plenty of meeting evaluation forms to be found on the internet but I favor an easy and effective way to evaluate meetings that I learned when I served on The Catholic Charities USA (CCUSA) annual gathering planning committee. At the end of the meeting, the chair would use a flip chart, draw a line from top to bottom in the middle of the page and label the top left "What Worked" and the top right "What Didn't Work" and then we would have at it.

- If it is in your power to cancel a meeting (that has no useful purpose) occasionally or altogether, do so. If you do not have the authority but have an opening to suggest (and the courage), do so.

- If it is in your power to shorten time allowed for meetings, do so. If it is not in your power, as above suggest it. Start with a 15-minute cut and if the agenda is covered, then cut more. Remember, there is a cumulative time saving (in this case 15 minutes for each meeting attendee).

- Have an agenda for meetings that is circulated in advance with prep materials also distributed in advance (so there is no delay while attendees read those materials at the meeting). Place the most important items at the beginning of the meeting and just in case you run out of time, place the least important at the end.

- Establish rules like starting and ending on time (do not recap for late attendees, as it wastes time, disrespects those that are on time and reinforces the bad behavior not only for the latecomer, but for others in attendance that may reason they can come late too). Having a rule that only one person speaks at a time helps to prevent distractions and improve communication. It may seem obvious, but I find it helpful to have a rule that attendees come prepared for meetings which means reading materials sent in advance and completing any homework from the prior meeting. Having and circulating minutes not only provides for a permanent record, but can help attendees be up to speed for follow-up at subsequent meetings. Having attendees turn cell phones off, as opposed to on vibrate helps to limit distractions (on vibrate the receiver feels it and can be distracted from the matter being discussed while wondering what the call was about). If there is a phone in the office, you might have it forwarded or set directly to voice mail during meetings.

12. **Revisit this chapter, from time to time, anytime you feel your control of your time is slipping (at which time you should do a new time management log, perhaps for just a week), but at least once a year.** Share the chapter with others. It will be mutually beneficial. Don't rely on this chapter to be the be-all and end-all on time management. Surf the internet from time to time, for a book or article on the subject, and for the latest "time management tips."

Have You Heard This One?

The first-grader asked his mother why Daddy brought home a briefcase full of papers every evening.

She explained, "It's because Daddy has so much to do he can't finish at the office and has to work nights."

"Well, then," said the child. "Why don't they just put him in a slower group?"

From Edwin Bliss's wonderful time-management book *Getting Things Done*

Chapter 11

Dynamic Learning Organization

Never Say Never

Never Say Never when it comes to education/learning. Be a part of a Dynamic Learning Organization. If you learn, you grow. If you share your learning and teach others, they grow. If others grow, that will stimulate you to grow. The cycle continues and yours becomes a dynamic learning organization.

"No more pencils, no more books, no more teachers' dirty looks" and "School's out forever" are some of the lyrics to Alice Cooper's song *School's Out*. There was a time in my life and probably yours too when we looked forward to school being over, to being done with education and moving on to the next phase in life. Well, I have some bad news and good news for you. The bad news is that school is not out, it's never out. You may or may not ever be in a classroom again, but you must continue your education. The good news is that school is not out, it is never out. You may or may not ever be in a classroom again but continuous learning will make you a better supervisor. Don't take my word for it. Management guru, Peter Drucker (2006, page 194) says "...every enterprise [organization] is a learning and teaching institution. Training and development must be built into it on all levels – training and development must never stop."

Change is Inevitable

There is an old saying "The only things that are certain in life are death and taxes." I would add there is a third certainty in life, change. Life at work will change. Instead of being a victim of it, through constant learning you can be ahead of it; you can shape it, maybe even control it. Spencer Johnson in his book *Who Moved my Cheese?* (Johnson, 2002, page 74) says "Change happens; anticipate change; monitor change; adapt to change quickly; change; enjoy change; be ready to change quickly and enjoy it again and again." He also warns us (2002, Page 46) "If you do not change, you can become extinct."

Let's take a stroll down memory lane. My first supervisory job was in 1972 as director of an adult training program for persons with disabilities. Phones had two or three buttons on them, one for each line so you could put someone on hold to take another call or use the intercom (yelling at the top of your lungs down the hall or run downstairs to tell someone they had a call). Copiers were just starting to be used but, copies were mostly made with carbon paper and Gestetner or Mimeograph duplicating machines. There were no desktop computers. I started my second management job in 1976 at St. Joseph's Hospital in Paterson. We were still dependent on carbon paper and NCR (three or four copies separated by carbon paper, you had to press hard). We actually did have an overhead paging system but email was a long way off. We could send messages and small supply items through miles of a pneumatic tube system throughout the building (picture that plastic tube at the bank drive-thru and the little container you use to make deposits and cash checks, miles of them, throughout the nine floors of the hospital). Couriers were needed to transport messages to other sites, and there was the US mail. Shortly after I arrived things changed. An early version of modern day copiers came out. In short order they were all over and Gestetners and carbon paper were phased out. Then came the first generation mobile phones. They were as big as office hand-sets and you did not have to worry about accidental butt calling, you had to pull out an antenna to make a call. Even then there were so many dead zones you often had to find a phone booth when your beeper sounded (What's a beeper, what's a phone booth?). Along came the desk top and email. Throughout this time there were great strides in the development of organizational theory, leadership and management theory, books to read, workshops to take, certifications and trainings to take to learn the latest theory or technique aimed at maintaining and improving skills and developing new ones. Quality Assurance came on the scene (more education and training) and morphed into CI, CQI and now PQI with all that training. And labor laws have proliferated, necessitating continuous learning about legal HR practices.

I offer the above trip down my memory lane as evidence of the importance of continuous learning. Over my 45 year career in management, change was a constant. The workplace and life in general were constantly changing. There were new ways of doing things and new things to do, positions eliminated and added. We had to continue to learn to keep up with, get ahead of, and shape change. Change will be a fact of everyday work life and life itself, this year, next year, and for years to come. If anything, especially with the advances in technology, the pace of change will quicken. So, be prepared. Always be a learner and help others learn too! I offer four resources for your continuing education as follows:

1. Read to Learn

Reading is the easiest, most convenient, and economical resource available for your continuing education. There are no tuition or registration fees, and it can be done at the time most convenient for you. While I recommend building your own personal library, if your personal finances won't allow for that, there is always the public library. If your library doesn't carry the book you want, it can search other libraries for you and arrange an interlibrary transfer. Your employer may already have a staff lending library, and if not, perhaps might start one if asked. If it is within your decision-making authority, you can start an office library, suggests purchases, even invite staff to suggest purchases. Besides books, journal subscriptions are relatively inexpensive and can be shared among staff (coordinate subscriptions with different people subscribing to different journals and sharing them). In all my positions, I was fortunate that the organization valued reading as an education resource providing a budget for books and journals. I always invited staff to recommend selections and sometimes allowed individual employees a dollar limit per year for book/journal purchases (with a rule that there would not be duplicate purchases). You can add book titles, perhaps a gift card to a bookstore or Amazon books, and journal subscriptions to your holiday gift list for family and friends.

Book/journal clubs are great. They could be voluntary or mandatory. Both are effective. Voluntary clubs frequently meet over a brown bag lunch in a quiet room and discuss a book (or chapter of a book) that all read. The group chooses the book (job related). Mandatory clubs can operate the same way but since management provides company time, management might assign the selection, perhaps related to an issue at work (e.g., conflict resolution, public speaking, applications of technology in workplace, or related to some new technology or program being instituted in the workplace). In some work situations I would rotate among staff having one person responsible for doing a two to three page book report or a one to two page summary of an article or book chapter. Circulate the summary to co-workers at least three workdays before the club meeting which takes place the last twenty minutes of the monthly staff meeting. The person doing the written summary would lead the discussion and all would be expected to read the material. Whether or not you participate in an office book/journal club, read on your own. If you read for even ten to 15 minutes a day, over the years, you will be quite well read. "You learn more by reading more" (Cottrell, 2002, page 86). If you used a portion of your lunch or coffee breaks, daily or a few times a week, this would easily be possible. And of course you could do this reading on your own time (just ten to fifteen minutes a day - and of course, more if you choose). "[Successful people] believe that books are a gateway to learning and knowledge." If reading as a pathway to success isn't enough to get you motivated, consider these health benefits of reading: Reading has been shown to help prevent stress, depression, and dementia, while enhancing confidence, empathy, decision-making, and overall life satisfaction" (Merle, 2016, page 1). How do you decide what to read? I recommend it be purposeful. Have work related goals. At least a part of your reading should be connected to your goals. I recommend you write your goals down. If you write goals down you increase the likelihood of achieving them. This is more than just my opinion; it is fact. Dr. Gail Matthews (Matthews, G., 2007) presented her paper *The impact of commitment, accountability, and written goals on goal achievement* at the 87th Convention of the Western Psychological Association, Vancouver, B.C., Canada. She conducted a study and found that just by writing goals down you were 42 percent more likely to achieve them. Further, she found that those who wrote down the goals, wrote down action steps to achieve the goals, and shared the goals and steps, were likely to achieve as much as 76% of their goals. You might set goals as part of your annual review, where on your own, directed by your supervisor, or a combination of the two, you settle upon written goals which will inform your decisions about topics for your reading. In addition to choosing reading material related to your goals, you should choose reading material related to circumstances as they occur or are anticipated to occur at work. If for example your organization decides to introduce a merit-based raise system, your employer will provide some mandatory training but there is no reason you couldn't do additional reading.

2. *Listen to Learn*

Listen to what others say to you and each other. Listen to what they say and what they do. Initiate such learning by asking questions of employees, co-workers, and supervisors using the skills covered in the communication chapter. You can learn from others' successes and failures if you observe and listen. There is a lot of knowledge, wisdom, and free advice all around you at work. The workplace can be a gold mine of learning so mine it. Ignore it at your own peril.

Most people drive to and from work. Some are lucky to have a short commute. Many have a long commute. Drive time can be very productive. I already suggested one productive use for driving time in the chapter on communication, that is, use it to talk out loud and practice an upcoming speech or remarks. Use some of your drive time to listen to self-help and management books. Select them in the same way I suggested selecting reading material in #1 above. You can buy CDs, check them out of the library, borrow them from work if they have any (ask your supervisor to add some to the work library), share among co-workers, and/or add them to your holiday gift list.

Other resources include online learning, workshops, lectures and trade shows, professional meetings or convocations, and of course, certificate/degree programs. Most often there will be costs associated with these choices. Perhaps your employer will pay some or all the cost. If there are out of pocket expenses you might be able to claim them as a business expense on your taxes. Your own personal membership or organizational membership in a professional organization may entitle you to free or reduced fees for some offerings. Frequently there are planned networking events at professional gatherings where you can meet peers and exchange knowledge with them. If there are no formal networking opportunities there are always informal opportunities at breaks, during meal times, in between, before, or after sessions. There are those formal (and expensive) opportunities such as certificate and degree or advanced degree programs. They may be necessary for job advancement. Some certificate programs may be relatively inexpensive but there will be some dollar cost as well as time commitment. Degree programs will be the most costly, but might be a worthwhile and necessary investment in your future. They too will necessitate a significant time commitment necessitating adjusting time use at work and in your personal life. As with your choice of the other learning resources covered above, these choices should be made in relation to your professional goal setting to maintain your skill and broaden skills and knowledge, keep up with and shape change, and opportunities for advancement.

3. Use Mentors or Coaches to Learn
Utilize the services of a management mentor and coach. Be aware that there is a difference between the two though both share a similar goal of improving the person being coached/ mentored. There is a wealth of information on the internet differentiating the two.

A coach is a person, outside the organization, employed by the organization to assist the employee in acquiring a particular skill, or piece of knowledge that will improve the employee's performance in that job. It is generally for a short period of time (days and weeks, maybe months). Skills might include memo writing, public speaking, or conflict resolution. The coach is recognized as expert in the particular skill he/she is engaged to teach. Think of baseball and the use of coaches. Pitching coaches are retired ace pitchers; batting coaches are retired batting champs etc.

The mentor is a senior management person, most often an employee of the same organization recognized as a successful manager/executive in his/her personal and professional life.

The mentor is a longer term role, generally nine months or longer and emphasizes building a trust relationship between the mentor and mentee. The mentor emphasizes the mentee's development for the future in the organization and beyond. The mentor assists the mentee with such matters as building self-confidence, work/life balance, understanding impact of personal life on work and vice versa, and self-perception.

Some of the confusion between the two roles is that a mentor can also serve as a coach and a coach can serve as a mentor. For the first time supervisor, he/she would likely be more in need of the assistance of a coach to help improve on existing skills needed for the job and learn new skills or knowledge needed for the current job. Frequently, a new or junior supervisor does not have the resources to pay for a coach and so looks to a senior staff member to be their mentor but one who would provide the needed coaching. Increasingly, organizations are implementing formal mentoring programs, but if they don't (or even if they do), you can ask a senior person to facilitate your growth and help acquire and/or improve specific skills.

4. Share With and Teach Others to Learn

Share with your direct reports what knowledge and skills you have and acquire. Ken Blanchard (2015, page 92) says it best "...if you find it useful, you will share it with others." A chain is as strong as its weakest link. If the chain is weak it will fail. If you think of your team as a chain, you will want it to be as strong as possible to assure its success and prevent failure. Don't be selfish and keep knowledge to yourself. If your team fails it will reflect on you. If it succeeds it will reflect on you, favorably. So be a coach to employees. Use what you know and are good at to help them. If you are good at a particular skill but another employee in your department is better, have him/her be the coach for that skill. Coaching others yourself and asking others to be a coach, will improve the functioning of the department, enhance your image among your staff, building respect and trust. In the process, not only will your employees learn and grow, so will you, resulting in you being better at what you do and better at teaching your employees (it becomes a good vicious cycle of learn, share, learn, and so on and so on).

In supervision, identify and build on employee's strengths. Make it a part of an annual personal goal setting process for each employee. Support their requests for learning and encourage, even mandate, that they avail themselves of the learning resources identified in items 1 through 3 above. If there is a budget for it, give books/journals as gifts or rewards. I have given books on self-care, management and leadership to my senior staff at Christmas time. Occasionally I have recommended particular books or journals to an employee at annual review time, and sometimes even given a book as a gift that I thought would help them work on a particular goal.

Creating and supporting a Dynamic Learning Organization is as much a part of the supervisor's job (Drucker, 2006, page 181) as hiring, firing, giving work direction and evaluating. If the above resources are utilized widely you and others will notice it. Yours will be a very positive, cooperative, collaborative work environment, the kind of workplace people will be reluctant to leave and the kind of place others will want to work – a Dynamic Learning Organization.

Chapter 12

Create and Maintain a Positive Work Environment

The Case of St. Vincent's

It was 1986. I had been the administrator of St. Vincent's Nursing Home for less than two years. St. Vincent's opened barely three years earlier and was still experiencing growing pains, putting systems in place and developing a stable work force. The building was an old hospital, not ideally suited in terms of lay-out for nursing home use. Much of the furnishings were hand me downs from its hospital days. The backbone of the home was its nursing assistant staff, the people who provided most of the personal care for the residents. The salary scale was low for all positions, especially for the nursing assistants and turnover had been high. St. Joseph's Hospital owned St. Vincent's. It committed to building a state of the art facility within five years. While residents and their families were pleased with the quality of care we had a high turnover of private pay residents looking for a more aesthetically appealing facility (though quite a few residents returned to us when they realized our quality of care was superior).

Things seemed to be getting better. The census had stabilized with the 60% private pay needed to break even. Salaries were still low but turnover too was way down. Then a union came knocking at the door attempting to organize our nursing assistants. My employer, St. Joseph's Hospital, hired a labor lawyer consultant to guide us through the organizing process and assure we did not commit any unfair labor practices which might have led to immediate recognition of the union. I did not have a great deal of experience working with a unionized workforce (but I had some). It is my belief that organizations

119

with a hostile or negative work environment are susceptible to union organizing. It was also my belief at that time that we had a very positive work environment at St. Vincent's and I could not bring myself to accept that employees were so dissatisfied and unhappy that they would want a union to represent their interests. Not only was that my belief, I had scientific proof to back me up.

A few months earlier the employees at St. Vincent's were administered the Work Environment Impact Scale (WEIS). I had secured a grant to further develop St. Joseph's Family Practice Residency Program. The grant made it possible to hire a consulting psychologist to administer the WEIS and then work with my administrative team to develop an action plan to improve the work environment. The results of the testing confirmed that the work environment was across the board, well above average.

The Labor attorney consultant advised that we delay the scheduling of a vote on representation. I resisted postponing indicating my preference to schedule the election at the earliest opportunity once the organizers produced evidence of sufficient interest to warrant an election. The organizing campaign ended abruptly because the organizers could not even come close to the minimum number of signatures of interest to call for that election. The work environment at St. Vincent's was a positive one where employees felt they were being treated fairly, were cared for, and were given the opportunity to address their needs and wants directly with administration (through their immediate supervisors) without fear of retaliation.

What is a Positive Work Environment?

A Positive Work Environment makes employees feel good about coming to work, and this provides the motivation to sustain them throughout the day (Poh, 2015). Says Poh (2015) "[Work environment] ... means everything that forms part of employees' involvement with the work itself, such as the relationship with co-workers and supervisors, organizational culture, room for personal development, etc." To Poh's list, I would add the physical environment (structures, layout, appearance, furnishings, and supplies, even climate as in temperature). Within such an environment there is ongoing transparent and open two-way communication, focus on training and development, frequent and timely positive reinforcement of good work, a spirit of cooperation and collaboration (teamwork), and a balance between work and personal life (if an employee feels he/she is ignoring personal/family life he/she will experience diminished work satisfaction).

How Does One Create and Maintain a Positive Work Environment?

Use the resources and information provided in the other chapters of this book. At St. Vincent's we had our Sacred Documents. Staff knew them and were expected to conduct themselves in a manner that supported them. A great deal of emphasis was placed on communication. Money was budgeted for education and training in all areas of the work-force, inclusive of training in communicating, active listening, decision-making, conflict resolution, conducting performance reviews, progressive discipline, ethics, time management, leadership styles, and more. MBWA was a big part of building a positive work environment at St. Vincent's. I was known to all employees, on all shifts. I was viewed as someone that walked the talk, someone they could trust. If you want to build, maintain and grow a positive work environment in your workplace follow these steps:

Building, Maintaining, and Growing a Positive Work Environment 12 Step Program

1. **Re-read chapter 1.** Acquaint yourself with the organization's sacred documents. Introduce them to your staff, making

certain they understand them, understand you are committed to them, understand you want and need their commitment to them, and that they will be held accountable for acting in a manner consistent with them. If your organization does not have all these documents, volunteer your services to your supervisor to assist in their development (if it is in your decision-making capacity, involve co-workers and direct reports in any such development). Of all the sacred documents, the mission statement is the most important. It is the statement of purpose or reason for existence and should be the driving and organizing force behind all decision-making. If there is no mission statement then develop one for your department. You cannot do this independently of the organization. You will need to consult with your boss (and he/she might need to do the same up the chain of command).

2. **Always remember that "the main thing is to keep the main thing the main thing" (Covey, 1989).** Covey's intent in repeating the words "main thing" three times is to maintain your focus on the main thing, that which is most important, your purpose, intent or goal, and not to be distracted by other things going on around you. I particularly like the way David Cottrell in *Monday Morning Leadership* (2002, page 36) applies the "main thing" concept to leadership development. I regularly use Cottrell's approach in my consulting work, as I did at work.

I want to show you how I utilized Cottrell's approach to the "main thing" by describing how I used it during a three week consultation for the Karagwe District Cooperative union (KDCU) in Tanzania, Africa in 2016. The KDCU is a coffee cooperative with over 70,000 coffee grower members. I was invited to provide consultation and management training for its board and senior management staff. After reviewing KDCU documents, the senior staff agreed the KDCU mission statement was in need of revision. So we tackled that first. I facilitated a collaborative process inclusive of board and management staff and unanimous agreement was reached on a revised mission statement.

I then introduced the concept of "main thing." In a meeting with the senior staff I wrote on a flip chart (Cottrell, 2002, page 36) "The main thing for the KDCU is: To work towards a better economic and social well being of KDCU members." I confirmed the staff understood the statement was the mission statement that the KDCU just adopted. I also confirmed the staff understood the mission statement as being a statement of the organization's purpose which should be the focus of everything the KDCU does, so as to advance and support the mission.

I then asked the question "If the main thing for the KDCU is to work towards a better economic and social well being of KDCU members, what is the main thing for each department of the KDCU?" I asked them to consider what and main thing each department should be doing to support the organization's main thing (mission). I stressed that everyone should know what the main thing is and use it as a test to remain focused in decision-making. Using a flip chart, we went through each of the seven KDCU departments and together came up with a written statement "The main thing for _____ is _____." The department head for the respective department spoke first. The other department heads in the room and the general manager (CEO) asked questions and made suggestions. For each of the seven departments, the director tweaked his original statement.

I then assigned homework to the department heads.

They were instructed to do the following:
- Convene meetings with their departments.
- Present the KDCU mission statement.
- Share the main thing statement for their department.
- Explain why they believed the main thing statement was the best statement of what the department does to support the KDCU mission and; to invite questions, to confirm all understood; and, to invite alternative suggestions and edits to the statement.
- Each department head made some edits to the initial department main thing statement and brought it to the general manager for discussion and approval.

When that was complete a one page listing of the KDCU mission statement and department main thing statements was circulated throughout the organization and posted in each department. Staff was informed in this way not only what their main thing was, but what every department's main thing was so as to help break down silos existing among departments, creating awareness of each other's functions, and increase opportunities for cooperation in support of the KDCU mission. The finished product appears below.

KDCU Mission

KDCU MISSION

Our Mission is: To work towards a better economic and social well being of KDCU members

KDCU MAIN THINGS

Note: The KDCU Mission is the Main Thing or Purpose for the KDCU. Each Department of the KDCU has its own Main Thing or Purpose and it supports the KDCU Mission. The Mission and Main Things drive what the KDCU does.

Finance and Accounts: To make sure KDCU has enough capital to generate profit and not have to depend on bank loans to operate.

Organic Project: Work for higher selling price for organic members' coffee and help members to improve and maintain quality and quantity.

Marketing: Provide coffee on time, follow-up on coffee advances with RPCs assuring advances used accordingly, and search market information for best prices.

Internal Audit: To make sure internal control systems are in place and followed.

Human Resources: Recruit qualified job candidates and support employees in fulfilling job responsibilities and following KDCU policies, procedures, and rules.

Factory: Process coffee to local & international standards guaranteeing consistently high quality coffee.

Projects & Investments: Explore potential KDCU investment projects, implement and supervise them for benefit of members & KDCU.

> Prior to retiring, I used this same process with staff, helping to create awareness of the Agency's mission and the roles each department played in supporting the mission. I told them that decisions about changing the way things are done, starting new programs, shrinking or closing programs, and very especially, budgeting decisions, should be measured against support of the agency mission and the department's main thing. I encourage you to go through this exercise in your own department occasionally reviewing it to be certain the main thing has not changed and use it to focus your own and your staff's work.

3. **Provide a safe and clean work environment and keep it in good repair.** Whether the building is brand spanking new, real old, or something in between, it should be well kept, assuring a safe workplace that is aesthetically pleasing and respectful of the dignity of staff and clients/customers. If employees feel respected they will be more productive.

4. **Provide employees clear work direction.** Review job descriptions at least annually (I always reviewed them at the time of employees' annual performance reviews). Tell employees that at any time during the year, if they feel their job has changed significantly, they should ask to have their job description reviewed. When giving work direction be specific as to your expectations such as volume, and deadline for completion. Be clear on work schedule.

5. **Provide employees working tools and supplies to do their job.** Budget for upgrades and replacements e.g., computers, phones, copiers. You cannot expect employees to have a project done requiring the use of a copier when the office copier is constantly breaking down. If there is a variety of software versions used by employees there could be difficulty sharing files. Support a learning environment (see chapter 11).

6. **Establish rules of conduct**. There likely will be rules of conduct in the employee handbook. If so review them with employees, make certain they understand them and be clear they will be held accountable for compliance. Add additional rules of conduct for your staff (being certain they do not conflict with the organization's rules) that you feel will enhance the work environment. Some rules I feel are important would include

- No yelling at staff, visitors or clients
- Treat everyone with respect (even if they do not treat you that way)
- Admit mistakes
- Ask for help when needed
- Offer help when asked and even when not asked
- Avoid gossip
- Tell the truth

7. **Realize you are their boss, not their friend.** If you are promoted from within, realize that things are different. You are no longer one of the guys/gals. As a staff member you were one of the passengers on the bus. With the promotion, you are now the driver. You are responsible for getting the bus to its destination. You are responsible for the bus, the passengers and anything in the bus. You need to be loyal to the bus company, so no gripe sessions with your employees, siding with them against the brass (you are part of the brass now). Remember this. It is nice to be liked and you can be liked. But if you place so much importance on being liked that you do not consistently treat employees fair and hold them accountable for their job, you won't be respected. It is more important to be respected than to be liked.

8. **Involve others in decision-making (see chapter 7).**

9. **Welcome conflict as a way for the organization to learn, grow and strengthen teamwork (see chapter 6).**

10. **Do not absolutely prohibit personal problems from the workplace.** This one may be confusing. For years I would tell staff that if they were having personal problems, they should leave them home. Eventually I learned such was an impossible. Encourage employees to maintain

a balance between their work and personal life. But understand that what happens outside of work can and will weigh on employees' minds while at work, leading to distraction and decreased performance. Encourage and allow employees to take time to address personal problems, connect them to the organization's Employee Assistance Program (EAP) if there is one. If there is not, suggest the employer offer one. Be supportive but also be clear on expectations and limits to your understanding – the job still needs to get done.

11. **Have a suggestion box.** Invite suggestions about the job, the organization and the workplace. Encourage signing suggestions so that you can speak directly to the person for further information. Consider publishing suggestions and responses. In some of my work settings I would publish a monthly list of suggestions (sometimes editing language) along with my response and always explaining my reasoning.

12. **Be a person of integrity and expect your staff to have integrity.** One who has integrity tells the truth, walks the talk, admits mistakes, does what he/she says he/she will do, does the right thing when it is easy and when it is hard, when being watched and not being watched (Who knows when you are being watched? If you are a person of faith, you believe you are being watched and someday you will get the results of your Matthew 25 test). Honesty is the best policy. If you are less than honest, even for good intentions, you need to keep track of what you said to whom. Ever get caught in covering up a lie? If you always tell the truth, you don't have to worry about being found out and you don't have to keep track of your lies. Why is integrity important? It creates a trust relationship between

you and those who work for and with you. The opposite of trust is mistrust and suspicion. If you are not trusted, you will be second guessed. People will start taking sides. The work environment will be weakened. Integrity can be recovered but it will be a long and painful process. So make it your personal mantra to do the right thing. And expect and hold employees accountable for doing the right thing. One easy way to know if someone has integrity is to ask yourself if your employees had to choose to do the right thing in a difficult situation, would they ask of each other "What would (your name) do?" (Hunt, 1998 page 188).

Chapter 13

Know Yourself (Self-Assessment)

Ask Others

I introduced what I call the Mayor Ed Koch School of Management philosophy in Chapter 9 Step 11 of my 12 step supervision program. Koch is remembered for the line "How am I doing?" I commend Koch's advice to you. Ask that question. Listen to and act on the answer. There are multiple ways you can ask this question.

Ask it directly or indirectly of your supervisor. Don't wait for your annual review. At your regularly scheduled supervisory meetings, update your supervisor on your work, specifically on your annual goals, and ask for feedback. If you do not have regular supervisory meetings with your supervisor, ask for one (at least quarterly, but preferably monthly). Use such feedback to develop corrective action steps and add progress reports to the agenda for subsequent meetings.

Use the service of coaches to help with specific skills. In your annual goal setting process (usually as a part of your annual performance review), you will be setting goals for yourself. You might benefit from the expertise of a short-term coach. For example, if you had as a goal to improve your skill at conducting annual performance reviews, you might ask the HR manager or a peer in another department who is recognized for this skill, to evaluate how you currently carry out the task and coach you to improve.

You might seek out the services of a mentor to help you grow over an extended period of time in your broader scope of responsibilities. Unless your organization offers a mentoring program, the cost associated with hiring a mentor may preclude you from accessing a mentor.

Another way to ask is to seek feedback at your department meetings (perhaps quarterly). You could literally place the question on the meeting agenda, "How am I doing?" Be advised though, that if you have not created and supported a positive work environment (which you will have done if you have been guided by chapters 1 through 12) it is unlikely you will get honest feedback. If you have created a positive and safe work environment, staff may tell you how you are doing even without asking. You may not always like what you hear, so be careful not to become defensive and never shoot the messenger. In fact, thanking the messenger will increase the likelihood of constructive feedback going forward.

Even though it may be difficult to implement I recommend the use of the 360° degree program. It is a popular organizational performance feedback program, gathering input from up, down, and across the organization. Most supervisors will not have the authority to implement such a program as it involves the entire organization, well beyond most supervisors' areas of responsibility.

In meeting with social work interns at St. Joseph's Hospital back in 1977, I informed them that I would be scheduling their final internship evaluations, when one brave soul asked when they got to evaluate me. That question led me to develop what I call my "Supervisory Expectations Questionnaire", an iteration of which I have used in every supervisory position I held until my retirement in 2016. A generic version of this form can be found below. Feel free to adapt it for your own use. Let me explain how I used it.

When using it for the first time with a group of direct reports, I tell them the story of where it came from. I tell them I am always interested in improving my management skills and welcome feedback. I advise them filling out the form is optional, as is signing it, however I encourage them to sign it, so that I can sit down with them, one-on-one, to clarify anything about which I am uncertain and to discuss their comments, suggestions and questions. I also schedule a departmental meeting to discuss and review findings in a more general way, and specify actions I will take on in the year to come as a result. Most often there was 100% participation and the overwhelming majority of employees opted to sign the form. I keep the completed forms year to year, looking to compare progress and look for trends. I time the distribution of the survey to be as far as possible from the employees' annual review date to minimize the possibility of the employees giving high ratings in hopes I will do the same for them.

Ask Yourself

Blanchard (2015, page 63) says "Take a minute: look at your goals, look at your performance, see if your behaviors [actions] match your goals." Blanchard's advice amounts to putting Mayor Koch's question to yourself, often. In the chapter on delivering communication I recommended the writing down of goals. If you have written goals with action steps and timeframes, you can easily sit down and assess how you are doing, adding goals and steps, deleting them, and slash or, amending them. It will also provide you information to share with your direct reports and your supervisor as to how the department is doing. If you are not working and building upon your strengths, start.

In the chapter on Time Management, the Third Step of my 12 Step Time Management Process is "Plan Your Day." That daily plan with the accompanying "to do" list can be a daily assessment of how you are doing. Towards the end of each day I would look at my daily calendar where I kept my appointment, deadline and to do list information. I would confirm that I was getting things done, especially priority things. I would ask myself what worked and what did not work. And when things were not getting done or did not work, I would plan changes in the days and weeks ahead. In asking the question what worked and didn't work, even when things got done, I occasionally decided there was a better way, and adjusted my plans going forward anyway.

The ABC Organization Supervisory Expectations Questionnaire

THE ABC ORGANIZTION **Supervisory Expectations Questionnaire**

ABC ORGANIZATION

SUPERVISORY EXPECTATIONS QUESTIONNAIRE

A. *To what extent do you feel the Supervisor is available for consultation and/or to discuss problems which may arise pertaining to your job?*

☐ Never   ☐ Infrequently   ☐ Frequently   ☐ Always

Comments: _____

B. *To what extent are you kept informed about what you need to know about your job?*

☐ Little or none   ☐ Less than satisfactorily   ☐ Satisfactorily   ☐ Highly satisfactorily

Comments: _____

C. *To what extent are you kept informed of changes and events in the ABC Organization?*

☐ Little or none   ☐ Less than satisfactorily   ☐ Satisfactorily   ☐ Highly satisfactorily

☞ *In reference to B and C, please check which sources you hear information from:*

☐ Your mail   ☐ Word of mouth   ☐ E-mail

☐ Department meetings   ☐ Other (please specify) _____

Comments: _____

D. *To what extent are you given the opportunity to exercise judgment in making decisions?*

☐ Little or none   ☐ Insufficient   ☐ Satisfactorily   ☐ Highly satisfactorily

Comments: _____

E. *To what extent do you feel you have impact into planning for the Department's work?*

☐ Little or none   ☐ Insufficient   ☐ Satisfactorily   ☐ Highly satisfactorily

☞ *Do you feel you should have more opportunities to impact into planning?*   ☐ Yes   ☐ No

F. *To what extent are you encouraged to work hard and do a high quality job?*

☐ Little or none   ☐ Insufficient   ☐ Satisfactorily   ☐ Highly satisfactorily

Comments: _____

G. *To what extent do you feel the ABC Org. tries to avoid waste and handle money and manpower wisely?*

☐ Little or none   ☐ Insufficient   ☐ Satisfactorily   ☐ Highly satisfactorily

Comments: _____

H. *To what extent are you treated as a responsible person capable of doing a good job?*

☐ Little or none   ☐ Insufficient   ☐ Satisfactorily   ☐ Highly satisfactorily

Comments: _____

THE ABC ORGANIZATION
Supervisory Expectations Questionnaire | PAGE 2

I. *To what extent do employees support each other to achieve team work?*

☐ Never ☐ Insufficient ☐ Satisfactorily ☐ Highly satisfactorily

Comments: _____

J. *Do you feel you are treated fairly in comparison to your co-workers?*

☐ Never ☐ Seldom ☐ Regularly ☐ Always

Comments: _____

K. *To what extent do your supervisor follows through on promised action?*

☐ Never ☐ Seldom ☐ Regularly ☐ Always

Comments: _____

L. *Do you feel your Supervisor responds quickly to your inquiries?*

☐ Never ☐ Seldom ☐ Regularly ☐ Always

Comments: _____

M. *Do you feel reasonable effort is made to provide for staff development?*

☐ Never ☐ Insufficient ☐ Satisfactorily ☐ Highly satisfactorily

Comments: _____

N. *Do you feel the department has a reasonable base of support from other department?*

☐ Yes ☐ No

Comments: _____

Do you feel the Agency has a reasonable level of support from the CEO?

☐ Yes ☐ No

Comments: _____

P. *If there are any further comments or suggestions, please add them below or attach another sheet.*

_____
_____
_____
_____
_____
_____

Signature _____ Date _____
[optional]

Learning Style

We don't all learn in the same way. Google "learning style." You'll find lots of different descriptions of learning styles and some short free tests to identify your preferred learning style. Peter Drucker, one of the giants of modern management, favors a four type model that I like. In "Classic Drucker" (2006, pages 7-9) he says people learn and work through reading, writing, talking, or listening. A reader is comfortable with lots of reports and emails, and being cc'd on emails. The writer takes copious notes, even if he/she gets a copy of the speaker's power point presentation. He makes notes on handouts, and writes reports for others because in this way the message is crystal clear. The talker likes to use the phone or walk around to strike up conversations, pick brains and share thoughts orally. The listener is in the minority and is hard to identify, as he/she generally sits quietly taking in what others say. The listener likes to analyze what is said by others and quietly come up with solutions. Once you know your preferred learning style, you may want to direct people to send you an email or report as opposed to stopping in to give you a verbal briefing. If you are a listener, your MBWA walks will afford plenty of opportunity for learning by listening. But if you are a writer, while walking around you may be sending yourself short texts with key words or writing down summaries of what you listened to. The point is to choose learning opportunities most suited to your learning style. Or adapt the learning opportunity to your style of learning, e.g., if you learn by writing but want to make good use of driving time, listen to the audio book and then dictate summary notes at the earliest opportunity. I will cover learning styles of other employees in the next chapter.

Personality Type

Have you heard the expressions "different as night and day, fire and ice, oil and vinegar, hot and cold?" These expressions are metaphors for personality differences. I write this section to make you aware that there are different personality types. Using just the metaphor "different as hot and cold," there are many personalities in the work place, probably as many personalities as there are employees, from very cold to cold, to hot, to very hot and all kinds of temperatures in between. Just as you deal with different temperatures differently, (e.g., wear warm clothing, gloves, layer clothes, even check temperatures), knowing your own and others' personality types can inform the manner in which you interact with and mix with them in the work place. As you grow and continue to learn, read more about this topic. As you learn more about personality types, your own, peers, supervisor and direct reports you will be better able to manage yourself and manage work relationships.

In the 1950s and 1960s, early organizational psychology described the type A and type B personality. The type A personality was described as the impatient, go getter, achievement-oriented person, while the type B personality was the easy going, relaxed person. Psychiatrist Carl Jung developed much of the theory of personality traits. Katharine Briggs and her daughter Isabel Briggs Myers developed the Myers Briggs Personality Test in the 1940s delineating 16 personality types, stemming from Jung's typology. Knowing what your own and others' personality types are enables you to anticipate how each other acts and reacts, and helps you improve the opportunities for creating and sustaining a positive work environment. It also allows you to be more deliberate in choosing people that will be working together, as certain types make very good partners, while others are much more likely to clash. If you have the opportunity to take the Myers Briggs test, take it. In the meantime, add this topic to your to do list to learn more about. An in-depth discussion of personality types is beyond the scope of this Supervision 1.0 Handbook. Add this topic to your reading list mentioned in Chapter 11.

Chapter 14

Know Others

Déjà Vu All Over Again

In this chapter I will further develop the topic "Know Others" which I introduced in Chapter 3 *Meet and Greet, and Get to Know*. In this chapter I will provide a more detailed rationale for getting to know your staff and agency and further guidance on exactly how to do it.

Why Should You Get to Know Your Employees?

During the 19 years I led Catholic Charities I was honored by many groups for "my accomplishments." But they were not solely my accomplishments. In my remarks after receiving these honors I sincerely thanked the many others that enabled the work to get done. One of my favorite lines when making such remarks was that I accomplished that work standing on the shoulders of (and then would fill in the credits of departments, even specific people that got the work done). Your success as a supervisor is "the result of your team...you get paid for what they do. You need your team..." (Cottrell, 2002, page 75). Cottrell further says that the majority of the work (perhaps 90% or more) is accomplished by your team and that it is the supervisor's job to help his/her employees grow, personally and professionally (2002, page 77). If you are going to help someone grow personally and professionally, you simply have to get to know them. In getting to know them you can begin building a positive working relationship which in turn will help in developing and maintaining the positive work environment covered in Chapter 12.

Knowing your staff enables you to help them grow. As you become aware of their learning style you can adjust your teaching style to match. As you learn their strengths and weaknesses you can adjust work assignments to build upon strengths, improve upon weaknesses and avoid workplace disasters. As you learn what their likes and dislikes are, you can personalize praise and rewards which will improve morale and productivity. As you get to know your staff a trust relationship will develop and staff will feel comfortable sharing what is going on outside of work which can impact what goes on at work (Wolske, 2014, page 1).

The bottom line is for your department to be successful; for you to be successful; you need to have employees willing to follow your work direction, to follow you. For this to occur, there needs to be mutual trust and respect. If there is mutual respect and trust, staff will feel comfortable sharing their problems and concerns. To build such relationships; to build that positive work environment; you need to get to know your staff. As well, you need to help them get to know you and each other.

Know Others 12 Step Program

Getting to know your staff is a never ending story. It is not a one-time effort. It is a continuous effort. Change happens at work and in staff's personal lives all the time. There will always be more to know, something to learn, about your staff. So never stop getting to know them.

Your efforts should be gradual and paced, balancing the need and desire to know against the stage of the development of trust between you and each individual staff member and staff members' comfort level in sharing personal and family information. While some people are happy to divulge personal likes and preferences, others will be reluctant, especially before or if they know and trust you enough to do so.

1. **Review what you learned about staff from the "Meet and Greet" process described in Chapter 3, building upon that information as you proceed on these next steps.**

2. **As you work these steps be guided by the resource information found in the other chapters of this book.** Apply communication skills resources covered in Chapters 4 & 5 as you attempt to get to know staff.

3. **Continuously work on building that Positive Work Environment covered in Chapter 12.** A positive work environment is characterized by mutual trust and respect. If there is mutual trust and respect staff will feel comfortable sharing information and problems, and asking for help.

4. **Inquire about job related information first (as opposed to personal family info).** You want to understand staff's roles, priorities, impressions of the workplace, pressing needs, and concerns. Inquire about the employee's history with the organization, how and when he/she came to work for the organization, what is his/her understanding of the organization's mission, qualifications for the job (education and experience (which you can ascertain from file review but nonetheless should ask to show interest in them), current and long term goals and aspirations. One good question to demonstrate you are interested in them is to ask how you can help them (Kimbell, 2010, page 75).

5. **A good starting point for learning such basic information listed in Step 4 is to review employee personnel records.** Much of this information can be found there as well as other family information as they provide benefits information and emergency contact information for the files. But as above you may want to ask the employee's such questions anyway to give them the opportunity to tell you and see your interest in them, and to confirm the accuracy of what is in the file.

6. **Make the use of one-on-one meetings with employees and MBWA as your modus operandi for conducting business.** One-on-one meetings provide a private atmosphere where utilizing good communication (and listening) skills conducive to mutual information exchange. Such sessions, absent distractions demonstrate the employee has your attention and are a sign of respect, both of which increase the likelihood of employee self-disclosure. Similarly, as you MBWA and encounter staff, ask some of the same and similar questions as listed in Step 4.

7. **As you start to feel comfortable in your knowledge of staff that is work related (as in Step 4) proceed to learn more about staff's personal lives.** Be observant of body language as you attempt this. If you sense they are uncomfortable respect their privacy; back off and try again at a later date. Just because you are comfortable does not mean the employee is. Personal life information includes but is not limited to spouse or partner, children, other relatives, religious beliefs, sports interests, recreation preferences and what they do for fun and relaxation, hobbies, community involvement, and vacation interests.

8. **Use opportunities as they present themselves to learn more about staff.** For example, as you MBWA if you approach two employees chatting about last night's football game, you could pursue a line of questioning confirming who won, what is the staff's favorite team and maybe springboard to other recreational interests. If an employee comes by your office to explain he was late because he was up all night with a sick child, you could find out if there are other family members simply by saying you hope the other kids don't come down with it and wait for their response. The next day you can ask that

same person how the sick child is doing. Such questions provide the opportunity to better get to know the person and show the person you are human and you care. One-on-one meetings will present similar opportunities.

9. **Encourage out of work opportunities where you and staff can experience each other in a social setting and take advantage of such occasions to ask questions.** Keep your ears open too taking in information volunteered by others, and or, overheard from conversations others are having. A great deal of questioning and sharing can take place at the bowling alley, a movie, a ball game, or casual dinner. Caution, do not be hovering over people as if spying (prying). Mingle and be a part of the conversations and see where it goes. Again, if you sense any discomfort in asking such information, back off.

10. **Similarly, participate in and encourage employee participation in company sponsored activities such as awards, luncheons, holiday celebrations, office birthday celebrations, community service activities (e.g., an organization sponsored day of caring).** Some supervisors might avoid altogether, or attend such events but not mix much with staff thinking it best not to impose. Quite the contrary, employees might think you feel "too good for them" if you avoid interaction. Taking opportunities to interact with employees practicing Steps 10 & 11 help to break down the boss/staff wall, show both sides in a different light, provide a great opportunity to learn about each other and show that the boss cares about them.

11. **Use technology.** Even though I am retired I am still sending birthday greetings to former employees. While working I added the birth date of my direct reports and

others to my daily calendar. Inevitably I get thank you responses indicating how appreciative they are that I care. Other information too can be recorded this way such as anniversary of hire, promotion, deaths, weddings, and more. By being aware of the anniversary of a sad occasion you can be supportive of the employee who might be preoccupied that day and benefit from your understanding and support. As appropriate you can share such information with others (like at a staff meeting announcing Joe's birthday, even having a cake). You might want to keep a data (cheat) sheet on each employee (and your boss). The cheat sheet might include employee family names and relations, important dates, education pursuits, food preferences, sports and recreation interests and hobbies. This information, in turn, could be use to dish out praise and recognition, and/or send appropriate cards and notes.

12. **Prioritize (at least once a year).** Make a list of five people you want to know better. Perhaps they may be crucial to the success of a new or pending project. Perhaps you want to better assess their understanding and commitment to the organization's mission, or their potential for taking on more responsibility or advancement. Perhaps you just feel you do not know them as well as you know other employees on your team. Using the above Steps, write down a plan to get to know them better (Kimbell, 2010, page 85).

Caution

In the second paragraph under the heading *Know Others 12 Step Program* above I used the words "gradual, paced, and balancing." Many, perhaps most people like to talk about themselves and their family, but not everyone. Some will want to get to know you first and build up trust before doing so and some will simply prefer to keep their personal business private. So use your communication skills. Listen to what employees say and observe their verbal and non-verbal communications and respect their privacy if they choose not to disclose personal information.

Know Peers and Boss

While it is important to get to know and build a relationship with your employees, that is not sufficient for the success of the organization or for you. Failures on the part of your peers or your boss can have an impact on the success of the entire organization, on your department, and/or on you. There is a degree of interdependence between departments (e.g., if accounts payable is not paying your supply bills on time, you might not have supplies when you need them). If you do not have a good relationship with them, they might not be there for you when you need them. Occasionally they may even throw you under the bus. It is important to get to know your peers and boss and build a relationship with them before problems arise.

The above 12 Step program minus Step 5 will serve you just as well in getting to know your boss and your peers. And of course the same caveat as applies to getting to know employees, applies to peers and boss. Early on be sure to ask them what their *Main Thing* is and share what yours is. With both parties but especially with your boss, ask how you can help him/her realize his/her *Main Thing*. Share what your *Main Thing* is and as the relationship develops suggest ways to mutually support the organization's Mission and each party's *Main Thing* work.

Chapter 15

Self-Care

What is Self-Care?

Self-Care is the continuous process of taking actions to establish, improve, and maintain optimal physical and mental health. Such actions seek to manage and reduce stress, satisfy physical and emotional needs, and build, improve and maintain positive relationships in life (at work, home, and in the larger community). Self-care activities help to maintain a balance between your work and personal life.

Why is it so Hard to Do?

Walt Kelly, creator of the comic strip *Pogo* coined the phrase "We have met the enemy and he is us" for his 1970 Earth Day poster. Substitute "I" for "we" and "me" for "us" in that quote and you will have the beginning of the answer to the question of why self care is so difficult for supervisors, from the front-line supervisor all the way up the chain of command to the CEO. The supervisor often is his/her worst enemy when it comes to self-care. Thinking about why self-care is so often neglected, I had a light bulb/aha moment as I was outlining this chapter. It seems so simple, yet in all the reading I have done and workshops I have attended, no one offered the following explanation.

Pretty much any definition of the word supervisor (at work) will include responsibility for skill development and the activities of their direct reports; assuring policies and procedures are followed; and assuring they have the training, supplies, and equipment to do their jobs. Most definitions state the supervisor is in turn accountable to the next level of supervision. These definitions talk a lot about care, as in caring for subordinates, caring about your boss' needs and wants. You will be very hard pressed to find a definition of supervisor that speaks to the supervisor's right and responsibility to practice self-care.

Placing the needs and interests of direct reports and the boss is implied, if not explicitly stated, as being the primary role of the supervisor. Supervisors are rewarded for acting this way, and what gets rewarded, gets reinforced and becomes a strong habit (caution: such a habit will be detrimental to your health). There are at least two other reasons why it is hard to practice self-care.

As an undergraduate sociology major I learned about the Protestant Work Ethic. The Protestant Work Ethic is based on the belief that hard work pays off; you get ahead, get promoted, get raises, have job security, are a success if you work hard. Rather than wait to get your reward in heaven, you get it in the here and now. In my Catholic schooling I internalized certain themes, like: we are all neighbors; we are all brothers and sisters; and we are our brothers' keepers. Most other faith traditions support these same themes. Caring for others, putting others first is second nature to most of us, as is putting family and self second to work. If you live by the Protestant Work Ethic you might be inclined to work until you drop, ignoring needs of self and family. If you live by the value of caring for others, as a bread winner, your emphasis is on hard work so as to provide for your family, and as a supervisor you may feel obligated to sacrifice your own needs and interests in favor of your direct reports

It seems to me, that one very important lesson was not fully communicated and did not take hold in that Catholic schooling. That lesson would be to remember that part of the Great Commandment which instructs us to love your neighbor (and staff) as yourself. For those not familiar with such teaching, the "Golden Rule" offers the same instruction, "do unto others as you would do unto yourself." The Golden Rule and the Great Commandment command us to self-care, placing it on equal footing with caring for others. The airlines get it; why can't we? Before take-off, the attendants review safety procedures, clearly saying that in an emergency, should the oxygen masks drop from the racks above, place the mask on yourself first before assisting young children or infirm travelers. They understand that you cannot care for others if you do not take care of yourself. You need to "put yourself first" (Richardson, 1998, page 12).

Why Self-Care is Important

Self-Care is your friend. If you are in good physical and mental health and if you maintain balance between the demands of your work and personal life, you are better equipped to care for others, and not just your direct reports. You will be better able to focus on the day's routine activities and any surprises that come your way. You will be better able to focus on the job and work more efficiently.

If you do not practice good self-care habits, you will suffer stress and anxiety, leading to burnout. You may suffer physical and emotional symptoms, sleeplessness, fatigue, G.I. symptoms, and loss of interest in aspects of the job. Minimally you will not be able to function at full capacity; you will likely make mistakes; fail to properly supervise and support your subordinates, and risk losing advancement opportunities, possibly even your position.

A Self-Care 12 Step Program

1. **Look in the mirror first thing after you get up and say "I will take care of my mind, body and spirit. I deserve it."** If you are in front of a mirror at other times during the day, repeat the mantra. While commuting to and from work, repeat the message to yourself.

2. **Eat healthy.** Do not just resolve to each healthy. Ask your doctor what a healthy diet should be for you or search the internet. Make a list of specific things you can do. Start

with one or two items, and as they become a habit, add another, and another and so on (I read somewhere it takes a good thirty days of consistent practice to adopt a new habit).

3. **Get a good night's sleep.** There is plenty of guidance on the web about how much sleep you should get each night and how to get that good night's sleep. You can always consult your doctor (your health insurance carrier may have a "free call-a-nurse or doctor program" for advice). Good advice is to avoid caffeine three or more hours before bedtime. As you get older you may avoid waking up to go to the toilet by avoiding all beverages several hours before bed time. A "sleepy time" tea might help you sleep, but may lead to a bathroom run. Darkening shades or curtains might help. Some people like to watch TV in bed until they are sleepy, but for others TV might give you a second wind, making it difficult to sleep.

4. **Exercise.** You can join a gym (doesn't do any good if you do not use the membership). It does not need to be rocket science. If you are doing something, then step it up a little. If, for example, you walk two or three times a week for fifteen minutes, gradually increase the length of time to maybe twenty and then thirty minutes, and from three to five times a week, maybe eventually daily. You can even do some of this walking at work. Take the stairs up instead of elevator. Park your car further from the door. Consider consulting a health provider before making any lifestyle changes.

5. **Limit alcohol intake**

6. **Stop smoking**

7. **Use your vacation time.** Vacation is a time to recharge your batteries. Recharging takes time. Some people will use all or most of their vacation time a day or two at a time. What happens if you don't fully charge an electronic device? It loses power sooner, or dies. Fully charge your mind/spirit/body battery. Take a substantial amount of vacation time at once. If the organization cannot do without you for two weeks, then you are doing something wrong (go back and re-read this book). My first boss at St. Joseph's hospital strongly recommended all management employees take at least one full two-week vacation each year for that very purpose. She insisted two weeks was a must for that battery recharging. I know in my case it took me the better part of a week just to unwind so I could better relax and enjoy the second week. Hint - if you take all your time in one or two day increments you will feel like you never left and staff will feel like you are never around. When on vacation, try to keep work out of sight and mind. If you need to call in or check emails and respond, limit yourself e.g., once a day at a scheduled time for no more than thirty minutes.

8. **Read for enjoyment and read self-help/self actualization books.**

9. **Make some time sacred for self and family.** For some of this time, or at other times, go off the grid (turn off electronic devices) and better enjoy personal and family time. Robert Wicks says it this way: "Come home often" and references James Joyce's quote, "Mr. Duffy [not me, just a coincidence] lived a short distance from his body" (2003, page 126). The phrase "Come home often" refers to more than a house. It refers to coming home to your inner-self or spirit as well as any physical space associated with

the comfort of home and family. His point is that self and family often are ignored and must not be.

10. **Do other fun activities.** Date night, movie night, plays, musicals, music. Go to a sporting event, even play sports, join a team. Maintain balance between work and personal time.

11. **Surf the internet for additional information on self-care and self care tips.** Join one of the online self-care blogs, and/or sign up for a self-care e-newsletter.

12. **Develop a written self-care plan and share with at least one person.** Sharing will increase likelihood of following through (Matthews, 2007). In fact, this person and you can be support buddies.

References

Blanchard, Kenneth H, and Johnson, Spencer, *The One Minute Manager,* New York: Harper Collins Publishers, 2015.

Bliss, Edwin, *Getting Things Done,* https://en.m.wikipedia.org/wiki/Ed_Bliss.

Cottrell, David. *Monday Morning Leadership: 8 Mentoring Sessions You Can't Afford To Miss,* Dallas: Cornerstone Leadership Institute, 2002.

Cottrell, David, and Harvey, Eric, *The Manager's Communication Handbook,* Flower Mound, Tx: The Walk The Talk Company, 2003.

Covey, Stephen R., *The Seven Habits Of Highly Effective People,* New York: Simon and Schuster, 1989.

CPP Global Human Capital Report, "Workplace Conflict and How Businesses Can Harness it to Thrive", July 2008. https://www.cpp.com/Pdfs/CPP_Global_Human_Capital_Report_Workplace_Conflict.pdf

Drucker, Peter F., *The Effective Executive,* New York: Harper Business Essentials, 2002.

Drucker, Peter F., *Classic Drucker: Essential Wisdom of Peter Drucker from the Pages of Harvard Business Review,* Boston: Harvard Business Review Book, 2006.

Effron, Marc, and Ort, Miriam, *One Page Talent Management: Eliminating Complexity, Adding Value,* Boston: Harvard Business School Publishing Corporation, 2010.

"Epictetus." BrainyQuote.com. Xplore Inc, 2017. 19 March 2017. https://www.brainyquote.com/quotes/quotes/e/epictetus106298.html.

Farmer, John, *The History of New Hampshire 1831,* NC: Stevens and Ela & Wadleigh,1831.

Http://www.ahajokes.com/off29.html.

Http://www.phrases.org.uk/meanings/death-and-taxes.html.

Http://www.tensionnot.com/jokes/office_jokes/100_bricks_job_hiring_process.

Http://www.laughfactory.com/jokes/office-jokes#sthash.XqskyGue.dpuf.

Hunt, Michele, *Dream Makers: Putting Vision and Values to Work,* Palo Alto, CA: Davies-Black Publishing, 1998.

Ivančić, V., (2014), *Improving the decision making process through the Pareto principle application,* Economic Thought and Practice, no. 2, ISSN 1330-1039, str. 633-656.

Johnson, Spencer, *Who Moved My Cheese?: An Amazing Way to Deal with Change in Your Work and in Your Life,* New York: Putnam, 2002.

Kimbell, Meredith, Hadden, Richard, and Catlette, Bill, *Rebooting Leadership: Practical Lessons For Frontline Leaders (And Their Bosses) in The New World,* Dallas: Cornerstone Leadership Institute, 2010.

Lazar, Richard, PhD. http://lazarachievementpsychology.com/ebook.

Lebedun, Jean, *Managing Workplace Conflict,* West Des Moines: American Media Publishing, 2008

Martin, Rev. Joseph, *Fr. Martin's Guidelines for Alcoholics, Part 1.* https://www.youtube.com/watch?v=o3hV1EZXCB4, 1976.

Matthews, Gail, (2007), *The impact of commitment, accountability, and written goals on goal achievement.* Paper presented at the 87th Convention of the Western Psychological Association, Vancouver, B.C., Canada.

Merle, Andre, April 13, 2016), *The Reading habits of Ultra Successful People.* https://themission.co/the-reading-habits-of-ultra-successful-people-d565b26f15f5

Morrell, Margot, *Reagan's Journey: Lessons From A Remarkable Career,* New York: Threshold Editions, 2011.

Peters, Tom, *Re-Imagine! Business Excellence in a Disruptive Age,* London: Dorling Kindersley Limited, 2003.

Poh, Michael, (June, 2015), *5 Characteristics of a Positive Work Environment.* www.hongkiat.com/blog/positive-working-environment/. June, 2015.

Richardson, Cheryl, *Take Time For Your Life: A 7 Step Program for Creating the Life You Want,* New York: Broadway Books, 1998.

Wicks, Robert, *Riding The Dragon: 10 Lessons For Inner Strength In Challenging Times,* Notre Dame, IN: Sorin Books, 2003.

"Winston Churchill." BrainyQuote.com. Xplore Inc, 2017. 19 March 2017. https://www.brainyquote.com/quotes/quotes/w/winstonchu111314.html.

Wolske, Kelly, 5 *Benefits Of Getting To Know Your Team.* https://
www.zapposinsights.com/blog/item/5-benefits-of-getting-to-
know-your-team. 11/05/2-14.

Bibliography

Blanchard, Kenneth H, and Johnson, Spencer, *The One Minute Manager,* New York: Harper Collins Publishers, 2015.

Bliss, Edwin, *Getting Things Done,* https://en.m.wikipedia.org/wiki/Ed_Bliss.

Career Press Inc., *The Supervisor's Handbook: A Quick And Handy Guide For Any Manager Or Business Owner,* Hawthorne, NJ: Career Press, 1993.

Carnes, Ken, Cottrell, David, and Layton, Mark C., *Management Insights: Discovering The Truths Of Management Success,* Dallas: Cornerstone Leadership Institute, 2004.

Colan, Lee J., *7 Moments That Define Excellent Leaders,* Dallas: Cornerstone Leadership Institute, 2006.

Cottrell, David, *Monday Morning Leadership: 8 Mentoring Sessions You Can't Afford To Miss,* Dallas: Cornerstone Leadership Institute, 2002.

Cottrell, David, and Harvey, Eric, *The Manager's Communication Handbook,* Flower Mound, Tx: The Walk The Talk Company, 2003.

Cottrell, David, *Monday Morning Mentoring: 10 Lessons To Guide You Up The Ladder,* New York: HarperCollins Publishers, 2006.

Cottrell, David, *The First Two Rules Of Leadership: Don't Be Stupid; Don't Be a Jerk,* Hoboken: John Wiley & Sons, 2016.

Covey, Stephen R., *The Seven Habits Of Highly Effective People,* New York: Simon and Schuster, 1989.

Cox, Billy, *You Gotta Get In The GAME: Playing To Win In Business, Sales, And Life,* Dallas: Cornerstone Leadership Institute, 2007.

Cox, Billy, *Zapp! The Lightning Of Empowerment: How To Improve Productivity, Quality, And Employee Satisfaction,* New York: Harmony Books, 1988.

CPP Global Human Capital Report, "Workplace Conflict and How Businesses Can Harness it to Thrive", July 2008. https://www.cpp.com/Pdfs/CPP_Global_Human_Capital_Report_Workplace_Conflict.pdf

Drucker, Peter F., *The Effective Executive,* New York: Harper Business Essentials, 2002.

Drucker, Peter F., *Classic Drucker: Essential Wisdom of Peter Drucker from the Pages of Harvard Business Review,* Boston: Harvard Business Review Book, 2006.

Effron, Marc, and Ort, Miriam, *One Page Talent Management: Eliminating Complexity, Adding Value,* Boston: Harvard Business School Publishing Corporation, 2010.

"Epictetus." BrainyQuote.com. Xplore Inc, 2017. 19 March 2017. https://www.brainyquote.com/quotes/quotes/e/epictetus106298.html.

Farmer, John, *The History of New Hampshire 1831,* NC: Stevens and Ela & Wadleigh, 1831.

Garry, Joan, *Joan Garry's Guide To Nonprofit Leadership: Because Nonprofits Are Messy,* Hoboken: John Wiley & Sons, 2017.

Geller, Ilayne J., Cottrell, David, *The Manager's Conflict Resolution Handbook: A Practical Guide For Creating Positive Change,* Dallas: Cornerstone Leadership Institute, 2008.

Harvey, Eric, and Ventura, Steve, *The 10 Commandments Of Leadership,* Flower Mound, TX: Walk The Talk Company, 2010.

Hesselbein, Frances, *On Leadership,* San Francisco: Jossey Bass Publishing, 2002.

Http://www.ahajokes.com/off29.html.

Http://www.phrases.org.uk/meanings/death-and-taxes.html.

Http://www.tensionnot.com/jokes/office_jokes/100_bricks_job_hiring_process.

Http://www.laughfactory.com/jokes/office-jokes#sthash.XqskyGue.dpuf.

Hunt, Michele, *Dream Makers: Putting Vision and Values to Work,* Palo Alto, CA: Davies-Black Publishing, 1998.

Ivančić, V., (2014) *Improving the decision making process through the Pareto principle application,* Economic Thought and Practice, no. 2, ISSN 1330-1039, str. 633-656.

Johnson, Spencer, *Who Moved My Cheese?: An Amazing Way to Deal with Change in Your Work and in Your Life,* New York: Putnam, 2002.

Kimbell, Meredith, Hadden, Richard, and Catlette, Bill, *Rebooting Leadership: Practical Lessons For Frontline Leaders (And Their Bosses) in The New World,* Dallas: Cornerstone Leadership Institute, 2010.

Kouzes, James M, and Barry Z. Posner, *Encouraging the Heart: A Leader's Guide to Rewarding and Recognizing Others,* San Francisco: Jossey-Bass, 1999.

Krempl, Stephen F., *Leadership ER: A Health Checkup For You and Your Team,* Dallas: Cornerstone Leadership Institute, 2004.

Lazar, Richard, PhD. http://lazarachievementpsychology.com/ ebook.

Lebedun, Jean, *Managing Workplace Conflict,* West Des Moines: American Media Publishing, 2008

Martin, Rev. Joseph, *Fr. Martin's Guidelines for Alcoholics, Part 1.* https://www.youtube.com/watch?v=o3hV1EZXCB4, 1976.

Matthews, Gail, (2007) *The impact of commitment, accountability, and written goals on goal achievement.* Paper presented at the 87th Convention of the Western Psychological Association, Vancouver, B.C., Canada.

Merle, Andre, (April 13, 2016), *The Reading Habits of Ultra Successful People.* https://themission.co/the-reading-habits-of-ultra-successful-people-d565b26f15f5

Morrell, Margot, *Reagan's Journey: Lessons From A Remarkable Career.* New York: Threshold Editions, 2011.

Muller, Wayne. *Sabbath: Restoring The Sacred Rhythm Of Rest,* New York: Bantam Books, 1999.

Myatt, Mike, (2012), *5 Keys of Dealing with Workplace Conflict.* https://www.forbes.com/sites/mikemyatt/2012/02/22/5-keys-to-dealing-with-workplace-conflict/#40c13a51e95c.

Nichols, Geoff, *Taking The Step Up To Supervisor,* West Des Moines: AMI Publishing, 1997.

Nietzsche, Friedrich, *The Twilight of the Idols,* London: Wordsworth Editors Ltd. 2007.

Palmer, Parker J., *Let Your Life Speak: Listening To The Voice of Vocation,* San Francisco: Jossey-Bash Publishing, 2000.

Peters, Tom, *Re-Imagine! Business Excellence in a Disruptive Age,* London: Dorling Kindersley Limited, 2003.

Poh, Michael, (June, 2015), *5 Characteristics of a Positive Work Environment.* www.hongkiat.com/blog/positive-working-environment/.June, 2015.

Richardson, Cheryl, *Take Time For Your Life: A 7 Step Program for Creating the Life You Want,* New York: Broadway Books, 1998.

Weinstein, Elizabeth, Ph.D., *Mentoring For Success,* Virginia Beach, VA: Coastal Training Technologies, 1998.

Wicks, Robert, *Riding The Dragon: 10 Lessons For Inner Strength In Challenging Times,* Notre Dame, IN: Sorin Books, 2003.

"Winston Churchill." BrainyQuote.com. Xplore Inc, 2017. 19 March 2017. https://www.brainyquote.com/quotes/quotes/w/winstonchu111314.html.

Wolske, Kelly, *5 Benefits Of Getting To Know Your Team.* https://www.zapposinsights.com/blog/item/5-benefits-of-getting-to-know-your-team. 11/05/2-14.

Thank you for reading *Being a Supervisor 1.0.* I hope you derived as much from reading it as I did in writing it. Please feel free to add your review of my book on your favorite online site for feedback. Should you wish to share any feedback directly or ask any questions, email me at: duffyj112@gmail.com.

**BUSINESS
BOOKS**

BUSINESS BOOKS

Business Books publishes practical guides
and insightful non-fiction for beginners and professionals.
Covering aspects from management skills, leadership and
organizational change to positive work environments, career
coaching and self-care for managers, our books are a valuable
addition to those working in the world of business.

**15 Ways to Own Your Future Take Control
of Your Destiny in Business and in Life**
Michael Khouri
A 15-point blueprint for creating better collaboration,
enjoyment, and success in business and in life.
Paperback: 978-1-78535-300-0 ebook: 978-1-78535-301-7

**Common Excuses of the Comfortable Compromiser,
The Understanding Why People Oppose Your Great Idea**
Matt Crossman
Comfortable compromisers block the way of anyone trying to
change anything. This is your guide to their common excuses.
Paperback: 978-1-78099-595-3 ebook: 978-1-78099-596-0

Failing Logic of Money, The
Duane Mullin
Money is wasteful and cruel, causes war, crime and

dysfunctional feudalism. Humankind needs happiness, peace and abundance. So banish money and use technology and knowledge to rid the world of war, crime and poverty.
Paperback: 978-1-84694-259-4 ebook: 978-1-84694-888-6

Mastering the Mommy Track Juggling Career and Kids in Uncertain Times
Erin Flynn Jay
Mastering the Mommy Track tells the stories of everyday working mothers, the challenges they have faced, and lessons learned.
Paperback: 978-1-78099-123-8 ebook: 978-1-78099-124-5

Modern Day Selling Unlocking Your Hidden Potential
Brian Barfield
Learn how to reconnect sales associates with customers and unlock hidden sales potential.
Paperback: 978-1-78099-457-4 ebook: 978-1-78099-458-1

Most Creative, Escape the Ordinary, Excel at Public Speaking Book Ever, The All The Help You Will Ever Need in Giving a Speech
Philip Theibert
The 'everything you need to give an outstanding speech' book, complete with original material written by a professional speechwriter.
Paperback: 978-1-78099-672-1 ebook: 978-1-78099-673-8

On Business And For Pleasure A Self-Study Workbook for Advanced Business English
Michael Berman
This workbook includes enjoyable challenges and has been designed to help students with the English they need for work.
Paperback: 978-1-84694-304-1

Small Change, Big Deal Money as if People Mattered
Jennifer Kavanagh
Money is about relationships: between individuals
and between communities. Small is still beautiful,
as peer lending model, microcredit, shows.

Readers of ebooks can buy or view any of these bestsellers
by clicking on the live link in the title. Most titles are published
in paperback and as an ebook. Paperbacks are available in
traditional bookshops. Both print and ebook formats
areavailable online.

Find more titles and sign up to our readers' newsletter at
http://www.jhpbusiness-books.com/

Facebook: https://www.facebook.com/JHPNonFiction/

Twitter: @JHPNonFiction